W9-CXX-130

THE ART OF CUISINE

Edouard Vuillard   *Museum of Albi*

Toulouse-Lautrec at Misia and Thadée Natanson's at Villeneuve-sur-Yonne, 1898

HENRI DE TOULOUSE-LAUTREC • MAURICE JOYANT

THE ART
OF CUISINE

Introduction by M. G. Dortu and Ph. Huisman

Translated by Margery Weiner

Culinary Notes and Annotation by Barbara Kafka

CRESCENT BOOKS, NEW YORK

ISBN 517 115751
Published in French in Switzerland under the title
« L'Art de la Cuisine »

Copyright © MCMLXVI by Edita, Lausanne

Translation, culinary notes, and annotation copyright © MCMLXVI
by Michael Joseph and Holt, Rinehart and Winston, Inc.

All rights reserved.

This edition is published by Crescent Books
a division of Crown Publishers, Inc.
by arrangement with Edita

a b c d e f g h

Printed in Switzerland

INTRODUCTION

Henri de Toulouse-Lautrec was convinced that cookery is an art. In fact, the art of painting was to him, first of all, an art of living. Thus, even after his withdrawal from society and his family's sporting life, which his illness caused, he became an artist without having to give up all pleasures. Being exceedingly fond of women his drawings of them were vibrating and thrilling, he painted horses with equestrian fervor and exactitude and as he adored good food he invented recipes with as much zest and unerring technique as he would put in decorating a menu card or painting a picture. He imagined a dish as an artistic creation, like writing a poem or dancing a ballet.

Today, Lautrec's fame, the high prices of his paintings, and the austere atmosphere of the museums in which we must view them, come between us and the exciting spontaneity of his masterpieces. They also make us forget that Lautrec enjoyed, in addition to his art, the pleasures of good friends, and good food.

Henri de Toulouse-Lautrec and Maurice Joyant had been childhood friends and their intimacy was renewed and deepened during the Montmartre years when Lautrec's fame was growing and when Joyant was director of the same art gallery in Paris which Theo Van Gogh had run before him. Lautrec was, throughout their relationship, the artist and innovator; Joyant, the steadying influence, the protector and, after the painter's death, the executor. Joyant created, after Lautrec had died, the Musée Toulouse-Lautrec at Albi, where most of the paintings which were in the artist's studio at the time of his death are now assembled.

However, it was their mutual love of food which was the true daily link between these men, rather than the more usual exchange of gifts or letters. In this sense, cuisine is a true memorial to their friendship. Thus, in the last years of his own life, Joyant collected the recipes invented in Lautrec's company, and combined them with the recipes that he and Lautrec had garnered throughout their years of companionship. He embellished the text with the Lautrec drawings and illustrations which illuminated this area of the artist's life. The book was published in a limited edition, and was conceived by Joyant as a work of art and as a tribute.

Now, a new edition of that original work is being presented to offer the dual pleasure of a collection of dishes that surprise and satisfy the modern gourmet, as well as a re-creation of the atmosphere that was so typical of Lautrec and his circle. Further, the present volume contains Lautrec drawings and menu decorations as he designed them to embellish his own dinners. The drawings facing pages 28, 32, 68, 88, 92, 100, 108, 112, 120, 132, 136, 140, 152 and 160, in this edition were used by Lautrec as menus or invitations. For the other menus, we have taken Lautrec drawings and used them as decorations in the joyful spirit of this artist-cook.

The result is an evocation of the Belle Epoque. Is there any better way, for example, to appreciate the Lautrec portraits of May Belfort and Cha U Kao than by cooking and eating the artist's incomparable ring doves with olives, created and cooked by Lautrec for only his favorite friends and models. (As a matter of fact, Lautrec used this dish as a judgement of character.) He would say of people he scorned, "They are not worthy of ring doves with olives, they will never have any and they will never know what it is." Such dishes, like the paintings themselves, reflect life in France at

Menu

a time when the artist could find the leisure to portray the world in his paintings, to paint it well, and also to eat well.

Lautrec and Joyant sought out and carefully recorded the recipes of "clever cooks and of conscientious mothers" in the same way that Lautrec had followed the lessons of Bonnat and Cormon. In London, Belgium, Spain, in every country where he travelled, Lautrec searched, not only for fine pictures, but also for any kind of new sensation and especially for a new dish or a drink previously unknown to him. His ardour, his curiosity made of him a hunter.

The artist also brought to his cuisine a marvellous wit. Who could forget the invitation to eat kangaroo in honor of an animal that he had seen at the circus, boxing a Negro (replaced at the last moment by an enormous sheep with an artificial pouch); or the house-warming of the apartment of his friends Natanson, in Avenue Foch where, in a crazy atmosphere, he managed to intoxicate all the artistic cohort of Paris, and launch the fashion of cocktail food?

Lautrec's interest in food and love of cuisine was a direct inheritance from his family. Like the other princes of the Grand Century, Lautrec's father and uncles loved sport, art, and food. For them, the hunt was an essential activity. Dinner was an important ceremony to be taken with serious and worshipful attention—an occasion not only to indulge one's love of food, but also to exchange ideas and pleasures with one's friends. These careful hosts kept wine for many generations; cheeses ripened slowly on their property; every dish was an invention drawn from a tradition tested through the years.

Lautrec learned from his family this domestic style in which the lord of the estate did not leave culinary matters to his servants but took a direct interest in the table.

In Lautrec's time, visitors were astonished to see that the artist's studio, in addition to being a workplace, was also a bar so well-stocked that he could offer them an infinite variety of cocktails— essential, according to him, for the proper contemplation of a painting. In Lautrec's view, every artistic expression should be accompanied by some culinary festivity, itself announced by a drawing, a lithograph, an elaborate menu. One ate or drank to celebrate a painting, a poster, an exhibition. Each working day was extended by a meeting in a restaurant, a café, or at home, where the menu was carefully composed. And these gatherings themselves became an occasion for new drawings—which in turn meant the sending of a decorated invitation or the drawing up of a list of courses.

Lautrec understood that the best meals are those that are well organized and, in addition, he attached great importance to the appearance of the table and the menu itself. He took great pains in presenting these menus to his guests, sometimes designing a totally new creation—a watercolor, a drawing, a lithograph. Sometimes he would transform or reproduce the theme or detail of one of his paintings. At other times he would adapt a lithograph primitively drawn for another use beforehand. He believed that a menu should be gay, witty, and in keeping with the atmosphere of the occasion.

Thus, painting was a part of Lautrec's daily life and cuisine was linked with his artistic being. When Lautrec was among his friends, travelling, on a holiday, or recuperating from the excesses of his life, the game of cuisine and painting continued. Often, Joyant and Lautrec spent their Sundays at Le Crotoy in Normandy, where they enjoyed fishing and hunting. Not only paintings, but also some excellent recipes have come down to us from those excursions to the seaside.

Whether in the company of other artists and writers, of music hall dancers, art dealers, or the intellectual bourgeoisie and the aristocracy into which he was born, Lautrec played the part of master in the enchanting game of culinary invention. One day, Edouard Vuillard even painted his friend standing before his oven. (This joyful portrayal is the frontispiece of this book.) How many ingenious gastronomic discoveries, no sooner made than forgotten, how many drawings, how many menus, how many rapid sketches which today are fought over by museums, were blown to the four winds after a joyous meal?

Joyant himself has written of some of these adventures:

"Around him, dishes and ideas proliferated: whether it was in Brussels, London, or in his habitual quarters of Paris and Arcachon, succulent and simple dinners were improvised in honor of the guests, the chosen of both sexes.

"Beyond this, outside of the cities, were the long hauls by sail, with heads in the clouds, when, as the only passengers on a cargo ship toiling through heavy seas between Le Havre and Dakar, we insisted, in full journey, on putting to shore on the coast of Brittany to inspect the fishing boats and to take on a cargo of lobsters and quivering fish. The boiler room was transformed into a kitchen. We opened cases of old port and fine olive oil . . . which, with premeditation, accompanied the baggage of these modern pirates who gorged themselves on vast lobsters à l'Américaine and Bourrides Bordelaises."

Lautrec, Joyant and their circle of friends lived in a milieu that was quietly free from social prejudice. They took their pleasures with all classes of society though, even with their love of novelty, they seemed to share a horror of excess, an evident predilection for subtle sensations.

For Lautrec, this happy and fruitful existence lasted scarcely more than ten years. Exhausted by excesses of work and pleasure, his feeble constitution gradually gave way, and following a crisis of *delirium tremens*, he was hospitalized at his family's request. Joyant, his faithful friend, saved him from moral breakdown, loaded him with new work, restored his taste for painting, and tangibly demonstrated the increasing success of the artist's work. However, this vigilant friendship merely offered a reprieve. Lautrec died in 1901, and after his death, the family entrusted his old friend with the preservation and protection of his work.

But it is the cuisine which remains a monument to friendship and to Lautrec himself. In 1930, Vuillard told the story of a memorable and succulent feast held in about 1897 at Lautrec's home in the Avenue Frochot—a feast somewhat mysteriously cut short at the cheese course: "Follow me," the master of the house ordered his guests, and led them a short way to the apartment of his friends, the musicians Dihau. Hanging on the wall was a then unknown masterpiece of Edgar Degas, inspired by the orchestra of the Opera where Dihau played the bassoon. It hangs now in the Louvre.

"There is your dessert," cried Lautrec, showing them the painting.

Paul Leclercq, the symbolist poet, has left us another simple portrait of his friend Lautrec:

"He was a great gourmand. He always carried a little grater and a nutmeg to flavor the glasses of port he drank. He loved to talk about cooking and knew of many rare recipes for making the most standard dishes, for in this, as in all else, Lautrec had a hatred of useless frills. And like a good Southerner, the more he valued straightforward cooking, the more he despised the doubtful and pretentious chemistry of restaurants and palace hotels.

"According to Lautrec, the exact amount of cooking, the quality of the butter and the spices, and a great deal of care, were the secrets of keeping a good table. He loved dishes which had been simmered slowly for hours and seasoned with perfect art. He tasted old vintages and liqueurs as a connoisseur. When he clapped his tongue against his palate and pronounced such and such a Burgundy to be like a 'peacock's tail in the mouth,' one was assured that the bouquets of the wine was fruity and rich.

"Lautrec cooked as well as he ate. Cooking a leg of lamb for seven hours or preparing a lobster à l'Américaine held no secrets for him.

"Knowing this liking for lobster, our friend, Georges Henri-Manuel once asked him to his home to prepare one of these shellfish. Apart from Lautrec, and of course, his faithful cousin, the doctor, I was the only guest.

"Georges Henri-Manuel was extremely thin and narrow-shouldered with a short black beard which broadened his cheeks, and according to Lautrec, made him look 'like a brush for cleaning the glass of lamp.'

"Henri-Manuel lived in a rather spacious apartment full of furniture and antique knickknacks, shined and polished with all the care that only a fanatic bachelor could give them. We arrived for dinner at the Rue François at the appointed time and our host first of all wanted to show us the kitchen quarters, where everything was carefully set out for making the famous lobster dish.

"Lautrec energetically refused even to put a foot inside. He declared his intention of preparing the lobster in the drawing room on an electric hot plate .... George Henri-Manuel, in great anguish because a lobster à l'Américaine has to be cut up alive, hastily covered his most precious pieces of furniture with sheets. Then, wrapped in a long white apron in which his short legs kept getting entangled, brandishing a spoon as long as himself, and moving saucepans about, Lautrec prepared the lobster à l'Américaine whose memory lingers with me yet.

"He took such care in the preparation that no damage was done to the drawing room and then, and then only, did Henri-Manuel breathe again."

In France, and for these people, food was a matter quite worthy of a man's and artist's intense interest, and was a special bond in the strong and lasting friendship between Joyant and Lautrec.

The recipes were devised and collected by men who loved eating. They are diverse in character, based on a firm knowledge of cuisine, and varied by solidly individual tastes. Lautrec and his friends actually prepared these foods and the recipes are, therefore, unlikely to be beyond the competence of any interested cook. They are presented here in their original versions, retaining their color of thought and language. The only modification are the notes that have been added to facilitate the work of food lovers in another time and in other places.

Thus, art, friendship, and food have come together in this book as the joyful legacy of Henri de Toulouse-Lautrec and Maurice Joyant.

M. G. Dortu Ph. Huisman

CULINARY NOTES

This book was written in an age when recipe books were exciting but rather imprecise and when the reading cook was expected to share the author's love of cuisine as well as his implicit know-how. Instructions were erratic. Measurement was generally vague and most of it was by weight or by liter.

The recipes in this volume have been left exactly as they were originally. However, notes have been added to most of them in order to make the recipes easy to use in the modern kitchen. Those recipes that do not have notes are either so clear that they do not need them, so vague in the original that the editor's note would be a complete invention, or so special that it seems improbable that they would be attempted—though, like all the recipes, they are fun to read. Often a recipe can give you ideas to try even if you don't follow it exactly.

The notes are not complete recipes, but must be read in conjunction with the recipes they follow. Unfamiliar weights and measures have been translated into standard American usage. English cooks must beware of measurements by the cup, as an American cup is only four-fifths of the size of those used in England. The English cook must subtract one ounce or three teaspoons for each quarter cup given in the recipe.

Measurements have not been listed for every ingredient that appears in the book, but only for those that are crucial. This is still a cookbook for artist-cooks and the quantities of spices, for example, have not generally been specified. They have been left to your imagination and to the frequent tasting of the food. The book does not attempt to teach you to cook, but if you can cook a little, you can follow the instructions.

You may find certain cooking procedures, terms, and ingredients in the text especially vague, unfamiliar, or confusing. These terms have been italicized in the recipes and you can refer to them in the list below:

Bind. One is often instructed to bind a sauce. This means that after the sauce is cooked, it is further prepared in such a way that it thickens somewhat and achieves a uniform and, generally, smooth texture. Binding is accomplished by adding an outside medium to the sauce: either a starch alone or in a mixture; or egg yolks, butter, or cream. Flours, such as rice and potato, starches such as arrowroot and corn, as well as the more usual white wheat flour, can be added to the sauce by first combining it carefully with a little cool liquid, either some of the sauce, water, wine, milk, or broth. Then stir in the warm sauce in small quantities until about a cup has been blended. Next, pour the blend into the remainder of the sauce and cook for about five minutes, stirring continually and not permitting it to come to the boil. Sometimes flour is kneaded with an equal quantity of butter and then this lump is permitted to dissolve in the warm sauce.

Egg yolks may be used to bind a sauce by beating warm sauce into them a little at a time until one half cup has been added for each yolk. Then return the mixture to the rest of the sauce and stir for about ten minutes over low heat. One has to be very careful to keep the heat low or the sauce will curdle. Reheating such a sauce is tricky for the same reason.

Use butter to bind a sauce by removing the sauce from the heat and stirring in a lump of butter until it dissolves. The sauce should be lukewarm rather than hot. It is the viscous quality of barely warm butter that does the trick. These sauces cannot be reheated effectively as the butter then melts entirely and the sauce becomes oily.

Binding a sauce with cream works on the same principal as binding it with butter, but is very complicated because American cream, even heavy cream, is much thinner than French cream. The English can use half clotted cream and half heavy cream, or, for a tart sauce, they can use half heavy cream and half commercially soured cream. Americans can proceed in the same way for a tart sauce, but are in difficulties with a bland or sweet sauce. They can either take twice the quantity of heavy cream called for in the recipe and reduce it by half over low heat or they can plan ahead and leave some heavy cream in a bowl in the refrigerator for two days and then skim off the heavy top part. People who can get non-homogenized milk can do the same thing, taking only the heaviest cream. Recipe notes in this book have been written to compensate for the problem.

Bouquet garni. This is generally composed of a few sprigs of parsley, a bay leaf, and a sprig of thyme. It is the most common herb-flavoring in French soups and stews. The herbs are tied together with a string so as not to get lost in the pot; they are removed before serving. In the absence of dried or fresh sprig thyme, a quarter teaspoon of dried leaves may be substituted. Other things, such as a clove of garlic or a sliver of orange peel, may be added to the bouquet qarni depending on the part of France in which the dish originated.

Cornichons. These are very small sour pickles or gherkins much used as a garnish and an ingredient. Occasionally, green cornichons are mentioned. These are the special cucumbers from which cornichons would be made. To substitute, use peeled, seeded small cucumbers, preferably slightly bitter.

Coulis. A coulis is halfway between a purée and a very rich broth. It may be made by cooking any specified ingredients until they almost liquify and can pass through a seive as a thick liquid. In a purée, on the other hand, all the solid matter is passed through the seive as well.

Court bouillon. A liquid used for cooking sea food. It is generally made by boiling the skin, heads, and bones of fish in white wine, or another liquid specified in the recipe, with the addition of vegetables and spices. The components of the court bouillon vary from recipe to recipe. Sometimes it can even consist of a liquid, spices, and vegetables, without any fish. For a really good strong basic court bouillon, take three pounds of fish odds and ends begged from your fish store, a bottle of white wine, plus enough water to barely cover the fish. Add one carrot cut in chunks, one medium onion, two stalks of celery, a small bunch of parsley, a few peppercorns, and a few cloves. Boil for about three hours, pass through a seive, and skim off any surface fat. Be chary of adding too much salt as many of the fish you may be cooking will have a salt content, especially if there is shellfish in the dish.

Cream. Especially that referred to as fresh cream (crème fraîche) is much thicker and fatter in France than the cream we buy in stores. (See entry *"Bind."*) All the notes have been adjusted to account for this fact.

Fines herbes. The group of herbs comprising this varies with seasonal availability and the dish. The base is parsley; tarragon, chives, chervil, or other leafy green herbs are used.

Fresh butter. This simply means unsalted.

Lard. This generally refers to unsmoked hardback pork fat, and is used either to insert in meat or to wrap it. Its purpose is to prevent the meat from drying out. Often bacon, unsmoked bacon, or salt pork is diced and added to a dish either plain, or previously browned in a frying pan. This adds flavor and substance to the sauce. Processed lard is unsmoked pork fat which has been rendered and is generally used as a fat either in sautéeing or in pastry. Lardoons are small slices or strips of fat pork or bacon inserted into meat in larding.

Meat glaze. This is the cooking liquid from beef, veal, and bones simmered in water, extremely concentrated by further cooking until a thick brown paste results. There are various commercial preparations of this type. The most widely known are very strong and do not compare with the homemade kind referred to in these recipes. They should be used in about half the quantity indicated in the recipes. A few specialty stores have a meat glaze made for them that corresponds to the homemade kind. The safest thing to do is to add the meat glaze gradually, tasting all the time. The effect of the meat glaze should be to add bass notes, to serve as a foundation that intensifies the meat inherent in the dish or sauce. If you begin to be able to identify the taste of the glaze, you are adding too much. If meat glaze is unavailable, one or two bouillon cubes will partially remedy the situation.

Paris ham. A boned, cooked, mildly cured ham. If very mild ham is not available, it is sometimes preferable to use a cooked uncured ham.

Reduce. To cook a liquid so as to diminish the amount. The higher the cooking heat, the quicker the reduction. If the sauce is delicate, however, it is better to use a fairly gentle heat. When not specified, reduce generally means to diminish the quantity by half, or until the liquid takes on the taste texture of a sauce. Reducing intensifies the flavor, therefore it is always wise to wait to salt and pepper a sauce until the reduction has taken place.

Roux. A roux is a thickening agent for a sauce made at the beginning of its preparation rather than at the end. It is composed of a fat, usually butter, and a starch, usually white wheat flour. Melt the quantity of butter called for in the recipe. Stir in, off the fire, the prescribed amount of flour. Make sure there are no lumps. If necessary, use a wire whisk to make perfectly smooth. Return to the heat and cook, stirring continually, for about five minutes so as to remove the raw taste of the flour. In most sauces, a white roux is required. This means that you cook over a low heat so as not to discolor the roux. If a brown roux is called for, use a high heat both to melt the butter and to cook the roux. Care must be taken to avoid scorching. Once the roux has been prepared the liquid may be added. If the liquid is hot, you must stir very briskly to avoid lumps. If the liquid is cold, you will have to cook for some time before the mixture thickens. You must stir continually, taking especial care to include all the mixture from the bottom and corners of the pan. It is often advisable to add the liquid in three stages so as not to have to cope with too much at once.

BARBARA KAFKA

ABOUT CERTAIN SOUPS

DE QUELQUES SOUPES

BEARNAISE SOUP

GARBURE BEARNAISE

In a tall soup pot put three to four liters of water, the leaves of a small cabbage—except the outer leaves—some potatoes, leeks, a turnip, a carrot, an onion, a clove of garlic, all well washed and cut small.

Let it boil, and add a good handful of dried haricot beans which have soaked overnight, a red pepper, a sprig of thyme, a little white pepper. Barely salt. Let it simmer on a low fire for three hours.

Three quarters of an hour before the cooking is finished, add a piece of *salt pork*, preserved goose, or duck.

When you are ready to serve, set some pieces of toasted bread in a soup tureen, and pour over them the soup, which ought to be fairly thick. Serve the piece of pork and the preserve separately.

This soup should be so thick a spoon will stand in it, using 8 qts. water, 4 medium potatoes, $1/4$ cup dried pea beans.

BEEF BOUILLON FROM THE POT-AU-FEU

LE BOUILLON DU POT-AU-FEU

Choose about three or four pounds of the shoulder of a good piece of beef, or hindquarter, in the sirloin; also three pounds of short ribs or bottom round; also some marrow bones. Preferably have a large earthenware stewpot. First of all put in the pieces of shoulder or sirloin—meat on the lean side; add the cut-up bones, with their marrow wrapped in a white cloth; poultry giblets, cold water—a liter and a quarter to a pound of meat—and a handful of coarse salt. This is to make the basis of the bouillon. One may add a piece of *salt pork*.

Place the stewpot on the fire, let it cook gently and skim.

After it has boiled for three hours, add the pieces of short ribs or bottom round—fat and tender—which are intended to make up the dish of pot-au-feu. Add whole carrots and turnips, a large onion stuck with three cloves, a clove of garlic, a quarter of a white cabbage previously blanched, a laurel leaf, celery, chervil, a *bouquet garni*, a few white peppercorns, and a pinch of nutmeg. Green cabbage and leek are not suitable because of their taste, unless they are very young—in any case, blanch them before cooking.

Let the pot-au-feu cook for another two hours and more. Take out the meat and the vegetables, skim the bouillon, which is easy to do when it is boiling; taste it to add salt and spice at your will; pass through a fine sieve and pour it over toasted slices of bread laid in a soup tureen.

The pot-au-feu is used as a family meal as set out in the recipe for beef from the pot-au-feu.

5 cups of water for each lb. meat; 2 lbs. carrots and 2-3 turnips.

PISTOU SOUP

SOUPE AU PISTOU

In a *marmite*, an earthenware soup pot, put six peeled potatoes, a pound of fresh red and white beans, a zucchini (green squash) cut in pieces, a large whole white onion. Moisten with water to the height of the vegetables, about two liters; salt; no pepper or *bouquet garni*.

Let it boil until the vegetables become a purée. Before it has finished cooking, add two beautiful large whole tomatoes; after a minute, take them out, peel them and seed them. Then, in a mortar, pound some garlic with one good plant of basil; add the tomatoes, some grated Gruyère or Holland cheese—a good quarter of a pound for six people. Make a paste by adding two or three spoons of fine olive oil and throw it into the reduced liquid of the *marmite*, removed to the side of the fire. Stir for at least ten minutes, then add pepper at the last moment.

Pistou is the basil paste; it binds the soup. Keep thick; cook on very low heat or cheese will separate out. One quarter-pound dry pea beans soaked overnight may substitute for fresh.

ONION SOUP

SOUPE À L'OIGNON

In a saucepan or, preferably, an earthenware frying pan, melt a pound of butter; when it is creamy, put in a laurel leaf and six or seven beautiful sliced onions. Let them brown while working with a wooden spoon until the whole is a good russet color. Add two spoons of flour and stir well so that it all becomes golden. Dilute with four or five liters of water or, better still, bouillon. Add a *bouquet garni*, salt, pepper; let it simmer and reduce to about three liters.

This done, at the bottom of a sauté pan, a soup pot, or a terrine with straight sides and flat bottom which can go in the oven, put a bed of grated Gruyère cheese, then slices of stale toasted bread, previously fried in butter and nicely golden; cover again with a bed of grated cheese mixed with freshly ground white pepper.

Taste the soup to add salt and pepper as you wish— on guard to remember that certain Gruyères are salted —and pour it, well strained and pressed, over the croutons.

When, after a few minutes, the croutons have risen to the surface, taste the bouillon again to season or to add salt if necessary, then cover with a layer of grated cheese.

Some people cover with bread crumbs mixed with parsley but this is a mistake because bread crumbs and parsley give a taste of their own.

Put into a hot oven, let it brown, and serve boiling.

4 qts. water or beef stock.

ONION AND GARLIC SOUP

SOUPE A L'OIGNON ET A L'AIL

In a large earthenware soup pot put about eight pounds of good butter and brown a good dozen large onions chopped fine and as many cloves of garlic.

Stir continuously with a wooden spoon while adding as much good wheat flour as the butter can absorb.

Salt and pepper strongly; continue to work this mixture as long as possible since it must become a paste. Turn this paste into a pot or into a tinned box with a tight cover and let it get cold.

With this preparation one can, in the high mountains, make about thirty soups, allowing a large spoon of the mixture per hunter.

Pour the spoonfuls into a *marmite* in which there is
boiling water from the glaciers or from the snow; let it
boil for a few minutes, then soak the bread, previously
toasted in front of the fire.

This soup is made to carry when hunters keep to the
mountains for a fortnight or so, and in the evening to
fortify people in a state of exhaustion, who are no
longer hungry but only thirsty, and who sleep out of
doors at altitudes of three thousand meters.

BORDELAISE FISH SOUP

BOURRIDE BORDELAISE

In a large *marmite* make a light-colored *roux* in which
you wilt *fines herbes*, parsley, water cress, fennel, chopped lemon, laurel, thyme.

Put in five pounds of common sea fish, with the heads,
cut in pieces: black conger, hake, whiting, homelyn ray
(cuckoo ray), red mullet, plaice, flounder, weever fish,
angler fish, red gurnet, stockfish. Add salt, white and
aromatic peppercorns, saffron, cloves and red cayenne
pepper.

Moisten with water to the height of the fish and let it
boil until the fish fall completely apart.

In the meantime, in this bouillon you will have
cooked, and removed from the pot, a whole choice fish
which is to be eaten: turbot, sole, brill, sea bass, had-
dock.

When the bouillon is reduced, throw in the following
paste made separately:

In a marble mortar crush five or six cloves of garlic;
add salt, an egg yolk, and, little by little, two or three

deciliters of oil, stirring continuously with the pestle to have a paste of the same kind as mayonnaise.

Let the fish bouillon simmer for another good quarter of an hour, then strain it and pour it into a deep dish over some toasted croutons. Serve boiling hot to go with the choice fish which should be eaten at the same time, like the beef from the pot-au-feu.

Roux : 3 Tbs. butter, 2 Tbs. flour with $^3/_4$ cup mixed, chopped, fresh herbs. Cook common fish (later thrown out) 3 hrs., place whole fish (to eat) on top; poach till done; remove; cook stock 1 hr. more; thicken with paste made with $^3/_4$ cup oil.

SPANISH SOUP

BOUILLON D'ESPAGNE

For a liter of consommé: put four liters of cold water in a stewpot made of earthenware, some salt, two spoons of lentils, a spoon of split peas, and a spoon of white haricot beans.

When the water boils, add a large leek cut in pieces, a hundred grams of carrots and a hundred grams of thinly sliced turnips, half a stick of celery, a piece of thistle, parsnip, and a lettuce cut in pieces.

Let it boil without a lid; then, with a lid; let it reduce on a low fire until one liter of consommé remains from the four liters of water.

Strain and serve hot.

This soup is excellent for intestinal inflammation and diarrhea and has the same properties as milk.

If one wants to eat it, without being ill, add pepper, salt, and a *binding* of butter with egg yolk and fried croutons.

FISH SOUP

SOUPE A POISSONS

In a large saucepan put leeks, tomatoes, and cut fennel, two laurel leaves, a few cloves, and some good olive oil. Brown.

Add some Mediterranean fish cut in pieces: rascasse, rock fish, hake, bass, head of conger eel—and let them brown lightly.

Moisten with water and let boil until the fish fall completely apart. Add saffron; strain the soup pressing some of the fish through. Cook some pasta in the stock and serve, adding salt to taste.

Rich, strained, fish broth—3 leeks, 4 tomatoes, a fennel, ¹/₄ cup olive oil, 2 lbs. cheap fish or 3 lbs. heads and bones. Cook 5 min. after adding enough saffron to turn soup golden.

MULLIGATAWNY SOUP

MULLIGATAWNY SOUPE

In a saucepan put a quarter pound of butter and twelve sliced onions and let them cook until they are brown.

Add twelve potatoes boiled to a pulp in water, one hundred seventy-five grams of flour, two large spoons of curry powder, two of curry paste, and three liters of very good bouillon.

Let it boil for an hour, skim the fat, add very small pieces of cold roast chicken. Serve boiling hot.

About 1¹/₄ qts. water for the potatoes—add more if needed. ³/₄ cup flour, 2 Tbs. curry powder, 2 tsp. curry paste, ¹/₄ lb. butter. Use 12 cups chicken bouillon and combine gradually, cold, with flour, before heating.

Menu

THE RAINBOW
OF
SAUCES

L'ARC-EN-CIEL DES SAUCES

WHITE SAUCE CALLED A LA POULETTE

SAUCE BLANCHE DITE A LA POULETTE

Put into a saucepan a good lump of butter and three hundred grams of a white *coulis* (made with veal, ham, onions, shallots, spices; reduced and moistened with bouillon, with four crushed hard-boiled yolks of eggs, with cream; the whole cooked and strained) or, in its absence, some very good bouillon. *Bind* with three yolks of eggs, add a pinch of scalded parsley, half a pound of mushrooms previously sautéed in butter, a quarter of good cream and let it heat. At the last moment add lemon juice, salt and pepper to taste, and throw sheep's trotters or other meats into this sauce.

Very rich. Use 3 Tbs. butter, 1$^1/_2$ cups of bouillon or *coulis* cooked for $^1/_2$ hour as follows: strong cooking juice of 1 lb. meat, 2 onions, 3 shallots, all chopped and cooked with 4 egg yolks, 2 cups bouillon, $^1/_4$ cup cream, and 1 to 2 Tbs. lemon juice. Combine butter and *coulis* or bouillon with yolks, etc., and 1 cup heavy cream.

PIQUANT WHITE SAUCE

SAUCE BLANCHE PIQUANTE

Cook gently in butter two onions, *fines herbes*, two cloves of garlic, tarragon, savory, laurel. Sprinkle with flour; moisten with a good white wine, a dash of vinegar, and fish stock. Add salt, pepper, spices to taste, lemon juice. Skim the fat and strain the sauce before serving with a pike.

Spice this sauce highly. Base it on 2 Tbs. butter, 1 Tbs. flour, $^3/_4$ cup wine and $^3/_4$ cup stock.

WHITE SAUCE, CALLED BECHAMEL

SAUCE BLANCHE DITE BECHAMEL

In a saucepan put butter and two spoons of flour; make a very light-colored *roux*; moisten with milk and work until it thickens to your liking; season to taste with salt, ordinary and aromatic pepper.

2 Tbs. butter, 2 Tbs. flour, and $1^1/_2$ to $2^1/_2$ cups milk, according to thickness desired.

WHITE SAUCE FOR ASPARAGUS

SAUCE BLANCHE POUR LES ASPERGES

Into a saucepan put butter and two spoons of flour; make a very light-colored *roux*; moisten with the water in which the asparagus were cooked and, at the end, add a large glass of good cream; season well with salt and pepper.

2 Tbs. butter, $1^1/_2$ cups asparagus water, $1^1/_2$ cups heavy cream.

YELLOW SAUCE CALLED "MAYONNAISE"

SAUCE JAUNE DITE MAYONNAISE

Put into a mortar one or two raw yolks of egg; salt; pepper; add a dash of vinegar and mustard; pour in fine olive oil, drop by drop, while stirring all the time in the same direction with a wooden spoon.

The sauce should "take" and become a paste. Continue until you have as much sauce as you want. Salt; pepper; add a little chopped parsley.

$^3/_4$ cup oil per egg yolk.

YELLOW SAUCE CALLED AIOLI OR MAYONNAISE WITH GARLIC

SAUCE JAUNE DITE AIOLI OU MAYONNAISE A L'AIL

Put into a mortar one or two raw yolks of eggs, three or four cloves of garlic—previously crushed in a napkin and then pounded to a paste—salt; pepper; a dash of vinegar or lemon juice; pour in, drop by drop, some fine olive oil, stirring with a wooden spoon always in the same direction.

The sauce should become the consistency of a paste.

Serve the aioli—the supreme Marseillais dish—with Icelandic salt cod, well desalted and boiled, with angler fish, with Mediterranean whiting—that is to say, hake —with brown snails or country snails (helix aspersa) or mourguettes—the local name for the white snails of the French South with black markings—cooked and seasoned, with mussels cooked in their own liquor, with pike and perch cooked in a *court bouillon*, with hard-boiled eggs, with potatoes, boiled or steamed, with young boiled carrots or cauliflower, with artichokes, Jerusalem artichokes, French beans, or asparagus and leeks.

$^3/_4$ cup oil per egg yolk. A garlic press and a whip facilitate success.

YELLOW SAUCE

SAUCE JAUNE

In a saucepan put six to eight raw egg yolks; mix them with a piece of butter as large as an egg, using a wooden spoon gently in a double boiler.

Go on working without stopping until you have firm paste. Take the saucepan off the stove, add yet another

Menu

egg-sized piece of butter, let it melt gently while continuing to stir. Add a good handful of chopped tarragon and a spoon of good wine vinegar and let it thicken.

Taste, add salt, and heighten the flavor with freshly ground pepper to taste.

Serve with all meats roasted over a fire of wood—kid, young goat, mutton, venison, etc.

About $1/_4$ cup butter for each egg-sized piece, $1/_4$ cup fresh tarragon or soak 1 tsp. dry tarragon in white wine vinegar $1/_2$ hr.

YELLOW SAUCE CALLED "MAITRE D'HOTEL"
SAUCE JAUNE DITE MAITRE D'HOTEL

Put in a saucepan a good quarter of butter, some chopped parsley, salt and pepper. Work and add to taste the juice of a lemon.

$1/_4$ lb. butter; barely heat to mix with juice; let cool.

YELLOW SAUCE
SAUCE JAUNE

Put in a saucepan three spoons of good wine vinegar with pepper, salt, laurel, thyme, spices, and let it reduce by more than half.

In a saucepan put a trace of warm water, add a bit of water to one or two egg yolks, butter or, if this is lacking, oil, the reduced vinegar, chopped tarragon, salt, and pepper. Work it well by stirring over a gentle heat or in a double boiler.

This is sauce béarnaise: careful—$1/_2$ cup butter per yolk, a bit at a time; 2 Tbs. fresh tarragon.

YELLOW SAUCE MOUSSELINE

SAUCE JAUNE MOUSSELINE

Put in a saucepan in a double boiler the yolks of four eggs; work them for two or three minutes. Melt separately one hundred to one hundred and fifty grams of butter and pour it warm over the eggs. Then, little by little, add slowly a quarter of a liter of cream. Go on working the sauce without stopping and it should thicken. When the sauce is sufficiently thick, add, at the end: salt, pepper, and, according to taste, nutmeg or cayenne pepper.

This sauce works. It may seem to separate at the end, or when reheating. To correct: remove from heat, beat hard with wire whisk. Use $^2/_3$ cup butter, 1 cup heavy cream.

DARK ORANGE YELLOW CURRY SAUCE

SAUCE JAUNE ORANGE FONCE CURRY

Put into a saucepan sixty grams of butter, a finely chopped onion, a bouquet of parsley on the stem, thirty grams of raw ham chopped into very fine pieces. Let it cook gently until the onion has dissolved.

Add a spoon of flour, and a spoon of curry powder; work and moisten while mixing in eight and a half deciliters of good stock. Let it boil for a quarter of an hour, then strain.

Put the liquid back to boil for a few minutes; then, with the saucepan away from the heat, *bind* two yolks of eggs and sixty grams of butter.

$^1/_4$ cup butter to begin, with 2 Tbs. finely chopped ham. 1 Tbs. each flour and curry. $3^1/_4$ cups stock. At the end, another $^1/_4$ cup butter.

YELLOW SAUCE, MOCK MAYONNAISE

SAUCE JAUNE, FAUSSE MAYONNAISE

Take four or six hard-boiled yolks of eggs, crush them and stir in well some good olive oil, adding one or two cloves of garlic, or very finely chopped onion. Salt; pepper; add to the flavor by such powdered spices as you like: sage, saffron, and a dash of vinegar or lemon to serve with fish. If you use this sauce with fish preserved in vinegar, leave the last ingredient out of the sauce.

A blender helps. Use from $1/_2$ to 1 cup oil, depending on number and size of yolks.

GREEN AND YELLOW REMOULADE SAUCE

SAUCE REMOULADE VERTE ET JAUNE

Add to sauce mayonnaise a chopped mixture of parsley, chervil, tarragon, capers, and cornichons.

Fresh herbs, quantities as in previous recipe.

SAUCE WITH YELLOW ORANGE WINE OR SABAYON

SAUCE AU VIN JAUNE ORANGE OU SABAIONNE

Mix well six yolks of eggs; pour in six small glasses of good white wine, or port, or sherry, and six spoons of sugar. Put it on the fire until the mixture thickens, stirring continually.

2 cups wine; double boiler, whisk, enormous energy needed.

GREEN SAUCE

SAUCE VERTE

Add to mayonnaise sauce: chervil, tarragon, parsley, chives, and watercress, all chopped and crushed very fine in a mortar.

Fresh herbs essential, in roughly equal quantities, about one-quarter cup, per cup mayonnaise. Can be puréed in blender. Whatever method, a thick paste is required.

ROSE-RED SAUCE

SAUCE ROSE-ROUGE

Incorporate in your sauces made of butter, bouillon, flour and *binding* also: tomatoes, cooked, strained and seeded; purée of sea-urchins' roe; purée of crabs' roe; butter—melted and passed through a sieve after having been colored with the cooking juices of prawns, female crabs, crayfish, lobster, crawfish, crushed anchovies.

WHITE AND GREEN SAUCE WITH CAPERS

SAUCE VERTE ET BLANCHE AUX CAPRES

Put into a saucepan butter worked with flour; moisten with the water in which fish has been cooked, or with plain water; stir while it is heating.
Before it boils, take the sauce off the heat; salt; pepper; add capers and, to taste, lemon juice.

3 Tbs. butter, 1 Tbs. flour, 1 cup water, $1/_4$ cup capers.

Menu

RED SAUCE CALLED "POOR MAN"

SAUCE ROUGE DITE "PAUVRE HOMME"

Put into a bowl two or three spoons of good red wine vinegar, parsley, onion and shallot chopped fine, no salt, freshly ground pepper. Serve cold with oysters and shellfish.

BROWN SAUCE

SAUCE BRUNE

To go with wild boar, venison:

Put in a saucepan a piece of butter, a shallot, three cut onions, two spoons of flour, and make a light *roux*; moisten with a glass of marinade if you have game; a glass of water; a glass of good red wine; a small glass of good cognac, and a spoon of vinegar. Add a *bouquet garni*, salt, pepper, a very large pinch of powdered sage if the sauce is to go with pork or wild boar.

Bring quickly to a boil; add, if you have them, the bits and pieces of meat from the game; let it reduce on a low flame without a lid for a good hour. If the sauce reduces too much, moisten with a little stock and some of the marinade.

When ready to serve, strain the sauce, which should be rich and thick, skim the fat and, finally, according to taste, incorporate at the same time as the skimmed gravy from the roast, two or three coffee spoons of the English sauce called Worcestershire.

3 Tbs. butter. ¹/₃ cup each marinade, water, wine. 2 Tbs. brandy.

BROWN SAUCE WITH MADEIRA

SAUCE BRUNE AU MADERE

Brown pieces of beef with onions cut in slices and laurel leaf.

Add a spoon of flour to give a rich brown, half a glass of *meat glaze*, half a Bordeaux glass of good Madeira, a clove; moisten with a glass of water.

Let it simmer for two hours, moisten with bouillon if necessary; strain the sauce; add salt and pepper to taste; add truffles, chopped and in thin slices, and previously cooked mushrooms.

Serve with a brown meat.

$^1/_3$ lb. shin of beef, 2 Tbs. *meat glaze*, 4 Tbs. Madeira, $^3/_4$ cup water. At the end, 1 to 2 truffles and $^1/_4$ lb. mushrooms sautéed in butter.

LIGHT BROWN ONION SAUCE
CALLED SOUBISE

SAUCE BRUN CLAIR A L'OIGNON DITE SOUBISE

Take a large handful of onions, slice them fine, let them cook for half an hour at a full boil; take off the stove and let them drain.

In a saucepan put onions, butter, salt, pepper; barely warm them, moisten with very good bouillon, let it reduce and pass it through a sieve, crushing the onions well.

This sauce can be added to a white sauce called béchamel.

3 medium onions, 2 Tbs. butter, $^3/_4$ cup bouillon. Reduce by one half.

BROWN SAUCE CALLED MIROTON

SAUCE BRUNE DITE MIROTON

Slice very fine a handful of onions, put them into a saucepan with a large nut of butter and let them brown. When the onions are very golden and creamy, add a spoon of flour; let them brown lightly again and cease-lessly stirring with a wooden spoon, moisten with good bouillon until it boils; add lastly a tablespoon of vine-gar, salt, pepper, nutmeg, cayenne pepper and let it reduce on a gentle fire for half an hour. Season to taste.

Without straining it, pour this sauce over the remains of boiled beef. Let it heat in the oven for a few minutes and serve very hot.

3 med. onions, 3 Tbs. butter, 1 Tbs. flour; 1^1/$_2$ cups bouillon and 1 Tbs. red wine vinegar, plus lots of seasoning to give a thick sauce for bland meat.

BLACK SAUCE

SAUCE NOIRE

Into a pan put a quarter or a half pound of butter and let it redden or, rather, brown. Take it off the stove and pour in two or three spoons of salted and peppered vinegar which has previously been cooked for a few minutes; garnish with chopped parsley and capers. Serve with hot fish, cooked in a *court bouillon*, such as pike, sea perch, skate, etc.

Brown butter carefully so as not to burn sauce. Must be served sizzling.

BROWN SAUCE WITH MUSTARD

SAUCE BRUNE A LA MOUTARDE

In a saucepan melt some butter, and then pour it into a warm sauceboat with vinegar, mustard, and chopped parsley. Work; salt and pepper to taste.

For each $^1/_4$ lb. butter, use 1 tsp. wine vinegar, 1 Tbs. mustard, 3 Tbs. chopped parsley.

BROWN SAUCE CALLED SPANISH

SAUCE BRUNE DITE ESPAGNOLE

Put in saucepan some ham, veal, carrots, onions, two cloves of garlic—all sliced—and give it a breath of heat; moisten with a wine glass of champagne and bouillon; add a *bouquet garni*, pepper, salt, lemon juice, and let it simmer for two hours. Lastly, add a good *roux* made in another saucepan and let it cook for another two hours. Pass through a sieve, skim the fat and use this sauce for whatever you think suitable.

$^1/_4$ lb. ham, $^1/_4$ lb. veal, 2 med. carrots, 2 med. onions; $^3/_4$ cup champagne, $1^1/_2$ cups bouillon. For *roux*, cook 2 Tbs. butter with 2 Tbs. flour slowly, until reddish brown.

MENU

ABOUT CERTAIN FISH, SHELLFISH, AND MOLLUSCS

DE QUELQUES POISSONS, CRUSTACÉS ET MOLLUSQUES

SALMON, TROUT AND COD COOKED UNDER THE ASHES

SAUMONS, TRUITES ET MORUES CUITS SOUS LA CENDRE

Have a trout or a salmon or a cod of about five to ten pounds; empty it carefully through the gills, wash and let it dry in the air.

Salt the fish inside and out; pepper; butter or oil the fish, and roll it in a wrapper of blackberry, strawberry, or wild raspberry leaves; tie it up with brambles if you have no string.

Then, having dug a hole in the ground, line the bottom with flat stones, take a large faggot of wood and make a large fire in such a way that there remains a big heap of ashes and embers.

Push the ashes to one side, lay your fish on the stones at the bottom of the hole, cover it with thin, flat stones and cover those again with the ashes and embers.

At the end of about twenty to forty minutes, according to the size of the fish, take it out, unswaddle it, and you should find the flesh of the fish deliciously cooked in the middle, although the skin is completely charred.

TROUT WITH CREAM

TRUITES A LA CREME

Have some trout preferably between half a pound and a pound each; empty them through the gills, clean and dry them carefully. Put a few peppercorns in the belly, make a few slashes in the sides, coat them lightly with butter; salt and pepper on the outside.

Put them on the grill over a charcoal fire and grill them like herrings.

This done, take a long, heat-proof earthenware dish, butter the bottom of the dish well; on it lay the grilled trout and cover them in such a way that the fish are well covered with good fresh cream worked with the green part of an onion—chopped very fine indeed—or, if you have no onion, with chives.

Put in the oven or leave over the charcoal, covering with a camp oven, and let them simmer on a gentle fire.

When the cream is slightly reduced and the trout ready to get brown, take out and serve hot in the dish as they are.

This dish requires a great deal of care so that too hot a fire does not cause the cream to curdle.

$^{1}/_{4}$ cup heaviest sweet cream and $^{1}/_{4}$ cup sour cream, 1 scant Tbs. chives or scallion greens chopped fine, per trout.

TROUT WITH VINEGAR

TRUITES AU VINAIGRE

Take a dozen trout freshly caught, empty them through the gills, wash and dry them carefully. Stuff the inside of the trout with peppercorns, four cloves, and some coarse salt.

Arrange the trout in an earthenware terrine which can go into the oven, and moisten to the height of the fish with good wine vinegar and a glass of good white wine.

Let them simmer for about twenty minutes; leave the trout in the terrine, bathed in their *court bouillon*.

and take the whole thing to a cool cellar to preserve it for at least a month in the summer and two months in the winter.

When you are about to serve, let the trout drain and arrange them on a dish surrounded by rounds of lemon and curled parsley. Each guest should garnish his trout with some good olive oil worked with a pinch of chervil and of finely chopped parsley.

This recipe can be used for herring, mackerel, and weever fish, freshly caught.

BRESLE RIVER TROUT

TRUITES DE BRESLE

Take some beautiful trout of about half to three quarters of a pound, empty them through the gills, clean and dry them carefully in a white cloth. Stuff the inside of the trout with shrimps, previously cooked and shelled, chopped and worked with some good butter; add a soupçon of tarragon or thyme, a leaf or a sprig.

Sew up the bellies.

Take some large vine leaves, wash them in cider, butter them lavishly; salt; pepper; envelop each trout in vine leaves and tie them up.

Cook them for a quarter of an hour in front of the hearth under the hot ash and embers; otherwise, put your trout on a grill in a dish which can go into the oven or under a camp oven.

Equal amounts of softened butter and shrimp—about $1/4$ cup each per fish.

TROUT AU BLEU

TRUITES AU BLEU

Have some black trout from the Black Forest or from our French mountains, carry them alive to the kitchen in a fish tank.

Boil some pure vinegar in a big pan or saucepan with a little salt and, as the trout are emptied and wiped in front of the fire, throw them in, still alive. The trout shrivel and become dark steel blue.

A few minutes' cooking is enough; arrange the trout, over which you have poured melted butter worked with salted and peppered chopped parsley. Garland the dish with rounds of lemon and little round potatoes boiled in water or steamed.

PIKE WITH RED WINE

BROCHET AU VIN ROUGE

Empty and scale a pike weighing four pounds. Wipe it, dry it carefully, and give it a few slashes across the sides.

In a saucepan make a *roux* with butter and flour; add half a bottle of good red wine, four to five cloves, a *bouquet garni*, aromatic pepper, ordinary pepper, salt, two or three whole onions if they are small, and a shallot.

Boil briefly.

On a long terrine or a dish which can go into the oven lay your pike on a bed made of a sheet of *lard* about as thick as a piece of paper. Cover it with the contents of the saucepan, add a nut of butter, and let it simmer gently in the oven until it is cooked, which ought to be in twenty to thirty minutes. The flesh should remain firm.

Arrange the pike on a dish and pour the sauce over it, strained, skimmed of fat, seasoned to taste with salt and pepper, and enriched with a good pound of mushrooms, separately cooked.

Encircle the dish with croutons sautéed in butter.

Roux: 2 Tbs. butter, 1 Tbs. flour. To bake: 2 Tbs. butter, 350° oven.

ROAST PIKE FROM THE SOMME

BROCHET ROTI DE LA SOMME

Having taken with cast and spoonbait a female pike of nineteen pounds three hundred and fifty grams, scale your fish, stick it with *lardoons,* anchovies, and slices of *cornichon.* Fill up the belly with a stuffing made of meat seasoned with spices; sew it up again and swathe the fish in slices of *bacon.* Put it on the spit before a big wood fire and pour over it some good white wine and butter.

At the moment of serving, untie and arrange the fish on a big dish, and serve it with a piquant white sauce made from the skimmed liquid. (*See* Piquant White Sauce for roast pike.)

The author is boasting. A smaller pike can be boned and stuffed with sausage meat; prepared as suggested and baked in 350° oven while basting with 1 part melted butter to 2 parts white wine.

PIKE IN PAPILLOTES

BROCHET EN PAPILLOTES

Have a four-pound pike, empty it, scale it, wash it
and dry it carefully.

Inside put salt, ground white pepper, and aromatic
peppercorns; swaddle it in a well-buttered white paper
and tie the whole thing up.

Lay the pike on two bricks in front of a wood fire,
on top of strongly glowing embers. Let it roast, turning frequently for at least a half hour.

Unwrap the pike and scratch off the charred parts.
Arrange the fish on a very hot dish and pour over it
some melted butter, seasoned with salt, pepper, and
worked with a small clove of garlic, some tarragon, some
parsley, and some chervil, all finely chopped.

**Less superb but more practical: wrap in foil, use 425° oven.
Sauce: about 4 Tbs. butter, 2 Tbs. fresh tarragon or 1 tsp. dry.**

PIKE A LA FINLANDAISE
FROM KAJANA, FINLAND

BROCHET A LA FINLANDAISE DE KAJANA, FINLANDE

Have a pike of three to six pounds, which is the best
weight.

Empty, scale, wash and dry carefully, cut the head,
open the pike lengthwise through the middle of the
belly, and lay it on a dish; pull out the central bone
which will bring the side bones with it in one stroke.
Finish cutting the flesh on the back lengthwise, and
then cut six, nine, a dozen steaks, according to the size

of the fish. Put the salted and peppered steaks onto a charcoal grill: just a breath of fire only.

In a large sauté pan put oil or butter, shallot, onion, parsley; let it brown slightly, and quickly throw in the fish steaks to finish the cooking and to gild them.

This done, arrange them on a hot dish, pour over them some good butter, melted separately, and worked with finely chopped parsley; add salt, pepper, the juice of a lemon, and serve very hot.

Tench can be cooked in the same way: to take away the muddy taste or to make scaling easier, throw your fish for three minutes into fast-boiling water.

Have fish store give you fillets with skin on. Slice into steaks. Without wood fire, begin immediately in saucepan, use $1^1/_2$ Tbs. butter per pound fish.

LEAN PIKE PATE

PATE DE BROCHET AU MAIGRE

For a two-pound pâté:

Boil your pike in a well-seasoned *court bouillon* the day before you want to make your pâté. Pound about three hundred to four hundred grams of boiled pike with fresh tarragon (if you have no tarragon use two spoonfuls of tarragon vinegar of wine), one hundred grams of fresh butter, pepper, salt, a few pinches of aromatic herbs prepared by pounding with a little coarse salt the following: a laurel leaf, a sprig of thyme, fennel, cloves, nutmeg, all reduced to a powder (do not use it all, only a few pinches).

Add two whole eggs to your pâté and mix it well. Take a pâté mold and line it with rolled out pastry;

next put in a layer of thin fillets of pike from which you have carefully removed skin and bones (the very nicest pieces of pike are kept for this). Add another layer of the pounded mixture, then a layer of pike and so on. Then, cover with pastry crust and make a chimney in the middle. Put it in the oven to cook for an hour and a quarter to an hour and a half.

Take it out of the mold and let it cool on a rack. Take away the chimney and through the hole put in a little concentrated *court bouillon*. Let it cool. If you use a terrine, butter it before filling it.

Begin with a 4 lb. fish. Use $^1/_3$ lb. or more for a paste with $^1/_2$ cup butter. Use a narrow mold. If pastry not desired, butter the mold and cover top with foil. Add about $^1/_2$ cup *court bouillon* that will jell when the pâté is tepid. Serve cold.

PIKE PATE AU GRAS

PATE DE BROCHET AU GRAS

For a two-pound pâté:

Boil your pike in a well-seasoned *court bouillon* the day before you want to make your pâté. Get yourself two hundred grams of sausage meat, six nice chicken livers or an equivalent quantity of goose liver, one hundred and fifty grams of mushrooms, one or two truffles, a few slivers of *uncured bacon*, a few sprigs of fresh tarragon, or failing fresh tarragon, a spoon of tarragon vinegar or wine.

When you have cleaned the mushrooms, chop them very fine; then, let them brown a little with butter until they have yielded up all their water.

Pound your tarragon in a mortar, then add the mushrooms which you will continue to pound until they are
reduced to a paste. Add salt, pepper, and finally the
liver and continue to pound a while. Clean two hundred grams of pike, taking out skin and bones, and,
separately, pound them also. Now add the sausage
meat, then mix it all up while adding a small glass of
cognac.

Round the bottom and the sides of your terrine
arrange thin slices of *uncured bacon*; then, add a layer of
paste; then, a layer of thin fillets of pike from which
you have carefully removed skin and bones; another
layer of the mixture, another layer of pike and so on,
interspersing the slices of truffle. On top put some
slices of *uncured bacon* and one or two spoons of concentrated *court bouillon.* Cover the terrine and put it
into the oven to cook for an hour and a quarter on a
small fire. Let the terrine cool with the lid removed and
take off the slices of fat on top.

JELLIED PIKE

BROCHET EN GELEE

Scale and empty a handsome pike the day before it is
to be eaten. Make a *court bouillon* with pure white
wine, cut onions, shallots, garlic, laurel, thyme, parsley,
fennel, clove, nutmeg, coarse pepper, aromatic peppercorns, allspice, dash of red pepper, salt.

After about a quarter of an hour's boiling, let it cool
and lay the pike in the warm *court bouillon*, which
ought to cover it completely. Let it simmer on a tiny
fire from twenty minutes to three quarters of an hour,

according to the size of the pike. Take it out and put it on a long, rather deep dish. Let the *court bouillon* reduce and mix it with the liquid from a calf's foot cooked with onions, shallots, carrots, salt, pepper, a *bouquet garni*—well strained, clarified, and skimmed of fat.

After having tasted it to perfect the seasoning if necessary, pour the *court bouillon* over the pike and let it cool to become jelled.

Encircle the dish with rounds of lemon and hard-boiled eggs; serve with a mayonnaise sauce lightly seasoned with Colman's mustard.

The calf's foot stock is for gelatin. If unavailable, cook 3 Tbs. gelatin with 1 cup well-seasoned broth; add *court bouillon* (made with 1 bottle wine) reduced to 2 cups.

PERCH WITH ANCHOVIES

PERCHES AUX ANCHOIS

Put the well-cleaned perch into a saucepan, bathing in equal parts of bouillon and some good dry white wine. Add a laurel leaf, two cloves, a clove of garlic, leek, parsley, sliced carrots, celery, fennel, thyme. Cook gently. Drain the fish and keep them hot.

Put the bouillon from the cooking through a sieve; work some butter in a saucepan with a little flour; let it brown lightly, moisten with the stock, and stir until your sauce is well *bound* and cooked.

Away from the fire, add anchovy butter—the weight of an egg—pour this sauce over the perch, encircle the dish with slices of bread fried in butter.

STEWED EELS FROM THE BRESLE RIVER

MATELOTE D'ANGUILLES DE LA BRESLE

Have some good eels of about three quarters of a pound to a pound and a half, from rivers of fast-flowing and clear water—downstream eels with pointed snouts rather than blunt.

Skin the eels, cut them into pieces about six centimeters long, and brown the pieces in a nut of butter on a very brisk fire with tiny onions and the beginning of their tender green cut in pieces two centimeters long. Add a spoon of flour.

When it is all well cooked and golden in color, wet it generously with a glass or two of cognac and let it flare. When the flame is out, add a large glass of white wine, either Burgundy, Epernay or any vintage which is a little dry. Salt; pepper; and let it simmer on a gentle fire, with the saucepan half covered, for a good quarter of an hour to twenty-five minutes, letting it reduce gently until the eel is cooked and the sauce rich.

Lay the pieces of eel on a white dish, strain and skim the fat off the sauce, season it to taste with pepper and with a drop of caramel to color it. Spread the sauce over the pieces of eel as well as the onions and their green. Surround the dish with small croutons sautéed in butter.

Have fish store prepare 5 inch pieces of 3 skinned eels. Use 3 Tbs. butter, 8 to 10 small scallions, 1 Tbs. butter, $^1/_2$ cup brandy, 1 cup wine.

Menu

FRIED MINNOWS

VAIRONS FRITS

Catch some minnows with bottles when they come out of a pure water stream or a fast-flowing river; press the bellies between the thumb and index finger, and empty them through the anus in one operation.

Wash them and dry them in a napkin.

Soak them in milk, roll them in flour and throw them into a fry of boiling oil.

Salt; pepper with white pepper or paprika, or red cayenne pepper; bless them with the juice of a lemon.

Lay the minnows on a dish wreathed with garden cress and serve very hot.

STEWED TURBOT LIVERS

FOIES DE LOTTE EN MATELOTE

Toward Christmas time, when the turbot come up-stream and are caught in large quantities in the eel pots, take a large dish of their livers.

Make a *roux* with butter and flour; when it is golden, add some very small onions with a little butter; let the livers brown slightly.

Moisten with equal parts of good dry champagne and bouillon, skimmed of fat.

Salt; pepper; add a *bouquet garni*; let it cook for twenty to thirty minutes.

Serve, garnishing the dish with little croutons sautéed in butter.

Cod livers can be used.

GRILLED EELS

ANGUILLES GRILLEES.

Have some eels from fast-moving waters of the Somme, of a maximum size of two fingers' thick. Skin them, empty them and cut them into three pieces.

Slash the pieces at the side, roll them in fine bread-crumbs and put them on the grill over a charcoal fire. Salt them as they grill.

Serve them with a brown sauce with mustard or with a piquant sauce with heated vinegar, seasoned with mustard and finely chopped parsley.

SOLE WITH TARRAGON AND WHITE WINE

SOLE A L'ESTRAGON ET AU VIN BLANC

On a tinned dish put a piece of butter about the size of an egg and a half. Let it melt until there is no more froth; arrange a bed of tarragon and lay on it a handsome sole which has been previously dried, and then brushed with flour. Salt; let it start on a brisk fire for about three minutes; then moisten with a glass of good white wine; cover with sprigs of tarragon and, on a brisk fire, let it boil for ten minutes to reduce. Turn the sole over.

Next put it in a very hot oven to reduce still further; pepper at the last moment and serve very hot in the dish.

The sauce should be rich and thick.

4 Tbs. butter, $1/_2$ cup wine for whole sole or 4 fillets.

PICARDY BRILL

BARBUE PICARDE

In an enameled earthenware dish make a bed of fresh butter scattered with aromatic peppercorns. Lay a brill out on it; salt; pepper; dot with butter and moisten to the height of the fish with good red wine cut with a third of water.

Surround the dish with a garnish of red gooseberries, previously scaled. Put in a hot oven, watch carefully, moisten, allow to reduce. Ten minutes before serving, cover with breadcrumbs and allow to become crusty.

This dish can not be prepared with a brill of less than a pound in weight and will cook, according to the weight of the fish, in from thirty to fifty minutes.

About ³/₄ cup gooseberries. 450° oven.

SOLE WITH WHITE WINE

SOLE AU VIN BLANC

In a well-buttered, enameled earthenware dish lay out a handsome sole, belly upwards. Dot with butter. Garnish with half a pound or a pound of mushrooms sautéed in butter, half a pound of shelled shrimp, a liter of mussels, half a liter of cockles—previously well washed, cooked, and removed from their shells.

Reserve the liquid from the mussels to boil it with the shrimp shells and some water. Pour a good glass of white wine over the sole and cover with the reserved liquid. Put in on the fire and let it simmer

uncovered for twenty to forty minutes, according to the
size of the sole, and let the sauce reduce. At the last
moment, dot the sole with butter, sprinkle with bread-
crumbs worked with parsley; salt; pepper; use very
little salt because of the already salted liquid of the
mussels.

You can work in the same way with all flat fish—
turbot, chicken turbot, brill, dabs, plaice and flounders
—working the other ingredients in the same proportion
according to the weight of the fish.

Whole sole or 4 fillets, 12-16 mussels, 6-8 cockles. Use $^3/_4$ cup
white wine, $^1/_2$ cup liquid from steamed mussels, $^1/_2$ cup water.
After shrimp shells have boiled, strain and cook sole in liquid. Add
sautéed mushrooms, shrimp, mussels, and cockles 5 min. before fish
is cooked.

BROWNED SALT COD BECHAMEL

MORUE BECHAMEL AU GRATIN

Take some nice fillets of salt cod, cut them in square
pieces and put them to boil in a saucepan full of water
in such a way that the water well covers the cod.

When they are cooked, drain and cut the flesh into
flakes while removing any bones, skin or cartilage.

Make a béchamel thus: heat a large spoon of butter
in a saucepan, add a good spoon of flour and let it color
on a very slow fire. Moisten with a liter of milk. Season with salt, aromatic pepper, ground peppercorn, a
pinch of nutmeg, and a dash of paprika.

Let it cook for a good half hour, stirring lightly with
a wooden spoon so that the sauce does not stick to the
bottom of the saucepan; mix the béchamel with the cod.

Menu

Take an earthenware dish which can go into the oven and garnish the edge of the plate with potatoes cut in slices and arranged into a crown (these potatoes should have been boiled already, but without falling apart).

Pour your cod mixed with your béchamel into the middle of this circlet. On top of this garnish with a thin layer of sliced potatoes or, if you prefer, of mashed potatoes, and cover the top of the dish with the remains of your béchamel sauce.

Sprinkle the whole dish with bread crumbs and a dash of paprika and of pepper. Put on top a few pieces of butter so that the bread crumbs do not dry out, and let it go into a very hot oven. Let it brown and serve hot on the earthenware dish and on boiling hot plates.

2 lbs. cod. Béchamel: 2 Tbs. butter, 2 Tbs. flour, 4 cups milk. 2 lbs. potatoes. 500° oven.

AIGO SAOU

Have some fish: perch, pike, bass (or only the first two), and mix them up. If they are on the large side, cut them into pieces.

In a large saucepan cook some whole large onions in salted water, a laurel leaf, a piece of orange skin, a little bunch of sage.

When the onions are almost cooked, add a fairly large quantity of medium-size potatoes which you have peeled carefully. If the potatoes are very large, cut them into two or four pieces.

When the potatoes are nearly cooked, add your fish which must cook according to its weight: five, ten, fifteen minutes, etc. . . .

Remove it from the fire.   Take a large deep dish and at the bottom put first of all the potatoes and onions, then the fish on top.   Chop together a lot of parsley and a clove of garlic.

Pour the cooking liquid into your dish so that it almost covers it.   Sprinkle with pepper, the chopped parsley and garlic, then pour over it some good oil and vinegar as for a salad.

With a spoon (without breaking the fish), mix this sauce well in your dish, covering the fish with it, and serve.

4 Lbs. fish (heads don't count in weight), 4-5 onions, 6 potatoes, $^1/_2$ cup finely chopped parsley, $^1/_3$ cup olive oil.

MARINE FISH BOILED WITH POTATOES

POISSONS DE MER BOUILLIS AVEC DES POMMES DE TERRE

Select among the numerous fish left behind at low tide on the sandy beaches of the Channel, such as cod, small skate, hake, red mullet, mackerel, plaice, flounder, sole, chicken turbot; empty them, scale them, cut them in pieces if the fish are too big, wash in several waters—especially the skate.

In a big soup pot put some peeled potatoes and sea water, or failing that, some water with coarse salt; let the potatoes boil and cook for a good quarter of an hour, then add some whole onions, a big *bouquet garni*, ordinary peppercorns, and the fish.

Simmer gently to finish the potatoes and to cook the fish until they are done, but in such a way that they do not fall apart.

On a very hot dish lay the pieces of fish, the potatoes, and the onions, moistened with the strained liquid. Pour over the whole some melted butter worked with parsley and finely chopped shallots, and a dash of vinegar. Sprinkle freshly ground pepper over it all.

STEWED FILLETS OF PORPOISE

FILETS DE MARSOUIN EN DAUBE

When mounted on the bowsprit of a cutter you have harpooned a porpoise in the English Channel, open it lengthwise and take from it some nice fillets of fish.

Scald them, stick them with *lardoons*, and let them brown in a pot with oil, garlic, onion, shallot, and flour; moisten with half a liter of water and half a liter of red wine; add salt, pepper, nutmeg, pimento, clove, and a *bouquet garni*; let it simmer on a small fire; add carrots and potatoes.

Skim before serving.

BISCAY SALT COD

MORUE À LA BISCAÏENNE

On a gentle fire in a copper saucepan brown leeks and cut onions, with some good olive oil.

Add some desalted cod, cut in very small pieces, a glass of good white wine, a *bouquet garni*, tomatoes—cut or in a purée—saffron, ordinary and cayenne pepper as you wish (no salt), a Madeira glass of good cognac. Flare, then fry some big pieces of cod. Put them in an earthenware sauté pan, pour over them the strained contents of the first saucepan.

Let the cod and its purée simmer for from five to ten minutes. Serve with fried croutons, rubbed with garlic, as you please.

To desalt, soak 3 lbs. salt cod overnight in cold water to cover. Sauce: cut small 1 lb. cod; add to 3 leeks and 2 med. onions, sliced, and sautéed in 4 Tbs. olive oil. Also add $^3/_4$ cup wine, 4 med. tomatoes (skinned, seeded and chopped) or $^3/_4$ cup tomatoe purée, 3 Tbs. cognac. Simmer 2 hrs. Fry 2 lbs. of cod in chunks. Press sauce through sieve and simmer chunks in it.

JELLIED DORADE
(SNAPPER OR SEA BREAM)

DORADE A LA GELEE

Scale, empty, and cut your dorade in pieces. Salt and let it marinate on a dish covered with a napkin for two hours.

In a cast-iron pot make a *roux* with flour and olive oil; add water, pepper, sliced carrot, one or two onions, one or two shallots, a stick of celery; boil and let it cool.

Then lay your dorade in the pot and moisten it to the height of the fish; let it simmer and cook for twenty to thirty minutes or so, and take out the pieces of the dorade to be restored to its original shape on a deep dish or in a fish terrine. Let the sauce reduce, pour it over the fish and, cooled, it ought to jell.

Carp and pike can also be prepared like this.

Begin by allowing 1 Tbs. flour, 1 Tbs. oil and 2 cups water for *roux* for each 2 lbs. of fish. After adding fish to pot add more water as needed to cover.

HERRINGS WITH ONIONS

HARENGS AUX OIGNONS

Have some white salt herrings from Boulogne-sur-Mer, preferably herrings with soft roes. Desalt them well.

Brown some chopped onions in a pot with one part butter, one part oil. In a separate pan brown the herrings in oil.

Next put them to simmer for a good half hour to an hour in a covered pot with the onions; add a nut of butter, a trace of salt, and some pepper.

Desalt by soaking in water 24 hrs. Use 2 onions, 1 Tbs. oil, 1 Tbs. butter for each pound herring. Finish with 1 Tbs. butter per pound fish.

SHAD GRILLED WITH SORREL

ALOSE GRILLEE A L'OSEILLE

Have a beautiful shad of at least three to four pounds, caught on the March high tide in the Loire or the Rhône.

Scale and empty with care. If there are any soft roes season them with salt and pepper and put them back in the belly; if there are hard roes set them on one side.

Split the shad lightly down the back lengthwise; put it on a dish and pour over it some good olive oil in which for twenty-four hours have been steeping onions, carrots, shallots—coarsely cut—a *bouquet garni*, red and white pepper, salt. Let the shad marinate for two to three hours and more, according to its weight, turning it over and pouring the liquid over it.

Put it on a grill over a charcoal fire or roast it in
front of a wood fire; turn it over gently and, when the
flesh sizzles, pour the marinade over it and dot with
good butter. When the shad is grilled to a turn, arrange
it on a dish and pour over it some good butter, melted
separately, and salted and peppered. At the same time
serve a large dish of young sorrel, girdled with rounds of
hard-boiled eggs. It is unforgiveable not to eat a fine
shad thus with sorrel which is its classic complement.

As for the hard roe put aside, brown them quickly in
butter; salt and pepper; add the juice of a lemon and
serve them hot on a crouton sautéed in butter; this is
an exquisite mouthful.

This can be cooked under a medium broiler flame.

BOUILLABAISSE

For six people one must have six pounds of Mediterranean fish of which three and a half pounds should
be rascasse (sea scorpion), two and a half pounds rock
fish—cuckoo wrasse, John Dory, gray gurnard or tub
fish, greater weever fish, angler fish, sea eel, bass,
whiting, chicken turbot, sole. One can add crawfish,
hairy crabs cut in pieces, and crayfish.

In a big wrought-iron saucepan forty centimeters in
diameter, put three quarters of a liter of fine olive oil;
two large mild red onions cut rather fine; two laurel
leaves; five cloves of Provençal garlic, skinned and previously crushed in a napkin to remove the essential oil
of the garlic; a bunch of parsley; some powdered thyme,
or rather the flower and leaf of thyme; a mustard

spoon of saffron; a soup spoon of coarse salt; a very
tiny pinch of cayenne pepper; five fresh tomatoes,
peeled, seeded, and chopped (if you have no tomatoes,
use three spoons of tomato purée); a strip of orange
peel; some dried, powdered fennel, preferably fennel
seed or a sprig of fresh-chopped fennel.

Stir and work relentlessly with a wooden spoon with
each addition until the oil becomes creamy and aromatic.

Put in the fish and whole shellfish or pieces of them
if they are too large. Mix, and turn them over so that
the whole is well impregnated with the oil, and let them
marinate for a good half hour—no harm will be done if
they marinate longer.

This process is carried out without cooking. Add
some freshly ground white pepper, continue to work
and set aside the few white fish which do not need long
cooking—bass, whiting, sole, chicken turbot, John
Dory.

To cook: Make a big clear wood fire—of vine cuttings if possible—so that the saucepan is completely surrounded by the flames which should meet above it.
Take care that the fire does not die down, particularly
toward the end of the cooking period.

Just as you are about to put it on the fire, moisten
with a large glass of water per head, in fact six glasses.
Look at the clock. Let it boil briskly for ten minutes
then stop it boiling by throwing in a glass of cold water;
let it boil again for three minutes and again throw in a
glass of cold water, to recommence the process of letting it go off the boil a second time; then let it boil again
for five to seven minutes.

In all, the boiling should take place three times in a
space of eighteen to twenty minutes at maximum, with

addition of eight glasses in all, which is enough to cook the fish and the shellfish; naturally, after the first boiling period of ten minutes, one has put in the pieces of reserved white fish—such as the whiting, sole, bass, turbot, and John Dory—in order that their flesh does not disintegrate.

This process of stopping the boiling twice and letting it start again three times is the whole secret of bouillabaisse; thus the emulsified oil amalgamates with the liquid and the whole is perfectly integrated.

Take the saucepan off the fire, quickly arrange the fish and shellfish separately on a hot dish. In another big, deep dish, on which you will have made a bed of slices of stale wheaten bread a centimeter and a half thick, pour the strained liquid, and let the slices steep in it. The remaining liquid goes over the fish and in a sauceboat.

Serve boiling hot because bouillabaisse has a horror of waiting or simmering, and must be sampled when it comes off a brisk fire.

Many fish unavailable; technique splendid; substitute 16 inch pot, 3 cups oil, $1/2$ tsp. saffron; begin with $4^1/2$ cups water; add $3/4$ cup water and again $3/4$ cup water and again $3/4$ cup water. Lacking roaring fire, use highest heat available.

BOUILLABAISSE

For six people, put into a saucepan two large mild onions and five tomatoes, cut up; four cloves of garlic previously skinned and crushed in a napkin; two laurel leaves; a sprig of fennel; a strip of orange peel; a clove.

MENU

Add half a liter of olive oil and let it barely brown, then add a good two pounds of rock fish, cuckoo-wrasse, rainbow-wrasse, sea eel, whiteheads, rascasse, chopped crabs, shells and feet of langouste, some angler fish; let them brown and render their liquid as they are being worked.

When it all begins to boil, moisten with a glass of hot water per head, season with salt, cayenne pepper, white pepper, and a mustard spoon of saffron. Let it boil for twenty minutes. Strain the liquid through a sieve, crushing the fish and shellfish up well, over another saucepan.

Put in the fish and shellfish which are to be eaten in order of precedence of cooking, the little langouste, one each, the prawns, the shrimps, the angler fish, the John Dory, the rascasses, the sea eel, the sole or the bass, and let it boil twenty minutes.

Arrange the fish and shellfish on a dish, strain the liquid over the slices of bread set out on another dish, and the remainder on the dish with the fish.

2 cups olive oil, $2^1/_2$ lbs. fish to give flavor and be thrown away. $4^1/_2$ cups water, $^1/_2$ tsp. saffron. Allow $^3/_4$ lb. mixed eating fish per person.

ENGLISH CHANNEL BOUILLABAISSE

BOUILLABAISSE DE LA MANCHE

This bouillabaisse is only a pale reflection of the bouillabaisse of Marseilles since it lacks rascasse and the Mediterranean rock fish which make both its basis and its savor.

Take some sea eel, angler fish or frog fish, hake, John Dory, ballan-wrasse, gray gurnard, sea bream, striped mullet, whiting, greater weever, dabs, plaice, chicken turbot, sole and, as shellfish, small crayfish, lobster, Norway lobster, crabs.

In a saucepan put some fine olive oil, tomatoes, cut pale red onions, and cloves of garlic skinned and crushed; let them brown slightly; add salt, white and cayenne pepper, laurel, fennel, saffron, the fish and shellfish whole and in pieces, according to their required cooking. Moisten with white wine and hot water and bring them to a fierce boil; then remove from the fire. As soon as boiling stops start it up again.

Carry out this operation three times running so that the fish has boiled fiercely for from fifteen to eighteen minutes. Thus it will be cooked and the stock integrated to one's liking.

Next put in a soup tureen some toasted slices of bread, pour over them some strained stock, and serve the fish and shellfish separately.

1 lb. fish, $\frac{1}{2}$ cup oil, 1 tomato, $\frac{1}{2}$ cup wine, $\frac{1}{2}$ cup warm water per person.

LOBSTER A L'AMERICAINE

HOMARD A L'AMERICAINE

Choose two fine specimens of lobster straight from the pots. While they are still alive cut them in two in the width; cut the shells again into two lengthwise, break the claws and the feet, and with the tails make some nice small rounds.   Carefully keep the liquid from these shellfish.

In a big sauté pan put half a pound of butter, two or three spoons of fine olive oil, two onions and a shallot chopped very fine; let it brown and get very hot, but without letting the olive oil boil.

When butter and oil are very hot, quickly throw in the pieces of lobster and let them brown on a good fire for about ten minutes.

This done, into a big saucepan pour the contents of the sauté pan and the reserved lobster liquid; moisten to the height of the lobster with boiling water; add a glass of good cognac, half a glass of good white Bordeaux, half a whole lemon, a large glass of very thick tomato sauce, a large glass of *meat glaze*, ordinary pepper, red cayenne pepper, salt.

Let it simmer for twenty to thirty minutes; take out the pieces of lobster and arrange them on a warm dish. When one has an abundance of lobster, increase the number of tails and claws to have more nice pieces, and continue to boil with the well-crushed shells.

In the frying pan with the strained liquid from the cooking in the saucepan, make the sauce by reducing further. *Bind* it with butter, a tiny quantity of flour, and season with red pepper, salt, and *fines herbes* chopped fine.   Pour the sauce over the pieces of lobster kept on the warm dish.

3-4 Tbs. oil, $^{1}/_{2}$ cup cognac, $^{1}/_{4}$ cup wine, $^{3}/_{4}$ cup tomato sauce, $^{3}/_{4}$ *meat glaze*. This sauce is useable for simmering extra lobster meat. Also add shells, cracked for flavor. Sieve sauce. *Bind* with 1 Tbs. butter for each cup reduced sauce.

As *Langouste Americaine:* this can be varied for different shellfish: shrimp, crayfish, small frozen South African lobster tails.

LOBSTER BONNEFOY OLD STYLE

HOMARD BONNEFOY A L'ANCIENNE

Have a nice lobster of about three pounds. Cut it into pieces while still alive—the tail in small rounds, the shell through the middle lengthwise; break claws and feet, set aside the liquid.

In a sauté pan put two hundred and fifty grams of butter, a tip of whole garlic, and let it heat gently. When the butter is boiling, take out the garlic, throw in the pieces of lobster, and let them brown quickly for about ten minutes on a brisk fire.

Next add a glass of tomato purée, two hundred and fifty grams of carrots cut in rounds, a *bouquet garni*, ten whole peppercorns, salt. Moisten with half a liter of very good bouillon, and let it cook so that it boils several times.

Now add two hundred and fifty grams of *meat glaze*, a glass of an excellent Sauterne, a small glass of very old eau-de-vie, and the liquid set aside from the lobster. Let simmer without a lid on a brisk fire for twenty to thirty minutes, letting the heat drop in the last few minutes.

While it is cooking, take two hundred and fifty grams of butter worked with thirty grams of chopped parsley and reserve; then two beautiful tomatoes out of which a thick *coulis* has been made separately in a saucepan, or have some ready-made tomato paste; reserve this also.

When the lobster is cooked, take out the pieces, arrange them on a dish put in an oven at very low heat, then strain the cooking liquid carefully and pour it into the saucepan containing the reserved purée of tomatoes.

Menu

Let it reduce in volume to a half to three quarters of a liter. Finally, when you are ready to serve, add, away from the fire, the reserved fresh butter and parsley, and pour this sauce over the pieces of lobster.

In this recipe there is no red pepper.

Variant of previous recipe. $^1/_2$ lb. butter, $^3/_4$ cup tomato purée, $^1/_2$ Tbs. carrots, 2 cups fish bouillon, 1 cup *meat glaze*, $^1/_2$ cup white wine, $^1/_4$ cup eau-de-vie, $^1/_2$ lb. butter with $^1/_3$ cup finely chopped parsley. *Coulis*: 2-3 tomatoes, peeled, seeded, chopped, and cooked to thick paste. Sauce reduces to 2-3 cups.

AMERICAN CRAYFISH

LANGOUSTE AMÉRICAINE

Have some Mediterranean crayfish of medium size, better on the small side; cut them into two lengthwise while still alive. Take the flesh out of the shells and set it aside as well as the liquid from the shellfish.

Let the pieces of crayfish brown in a saucepan with oil and onions. Add half a bottle of white wine and let it reduce almost entirely.

This done, add a *coulis* made separately—of a thin essence of beef, tomato, and onion, browned in oil with a trace of flour, a glass and a half of bouillon or *meat glaze* and some tomato purée, all well strained.

Let the crayfish cook for about twenty minutes, adding garlic, chopped parsley, the inside of the crayfish crushed and strained, as well as their liquid which had been set on one side.

Finally, pepper with red cayenne pepper, and salt. Serve very hot.

BORDELAIS CRAYFISH

ECREVISSES A LA BORDELAISE

Have some very lively fresh water crayfish and clean them carefully. In a saucepan put some butter, an onion, a carrot, and two finely chopped shallots. Throw in the crayfish and let them cook lightly. Add a small glass of Madeira or good white wine, salt, ordinary and cayenne pepper.

Let them flare and cook for about ten minutes. Remove the shrimps and arrange them on a deep dish; keep warm. Add to the cooking liquid either some bouillon or *meat glaze*, let it reduce, then strain it and *bind* the sauce with egg yolks and fresh butter. Add the juice of a lemon and pour the sauce over the crayfish.

2$^1/_2$ lbs. crayfish, $^1/_3$ cup cognac, $^3/_4$ cup Madeira or white wine, $^1/_2$ cup stock or $^1/_3$ cup *meat glaze*, 2 egg yolks, 2 Tbs. butter.

SCALLOPS

COQUILLES SAINT-JACQUES

Take some scallops. Clean the outside, open the shells, take out the mollusks, taking care to remove the black pocket at once. Wash in a lot of water several times to get rid of the sand.

In a *court bouillon* already made of sea water (if you have none, then salted water), carrots, onions, shallots, garlic, all chopped fine, laurel leaves, a *bouquet garni*, white and black peppercorns, a spoon of vinegar—put the mollusks to cook for about ten minutes, starting cold.

Take them out of the *court bouillon*, dice them, and fill the empty shells with them; two mollusks are necessary to fill one shell.

On these pieces of mollusk, pour a white Poulette sauce, enriched with mushrooms previously fried in butter, and mussels opened over the fire and dry.

Poulette Sauce will be found in the chapter on sauces; it is a white sauce, mixed with the liquid from the *court bouillon*, bound with an egg yolk and seasoned to taste with salt, ordinary and cayenne pepper, and the juice of a lemon.

Cover the shells with a little breadcrumbs dotted with butter. Put them in the oven and let them brown.

Allow per person: $^1/_2$ lb. scallop meat, or 2 entire scallops, $^1/_2$ cup sauce and $^1/_4$ lb. sliced mushrooms warmed in butter.

ARDENNES CRAYFISH

ECREVISSES DES ARDENNES

Have some very lively fresh water crayfish. Clean them carefully. In a saucepan lay a bed of parsley on the stalk, onions and cloves of minced garlic, and put the crayfish on top; sprinkle with salt, add some black and white peppercorns, cayenne pepper to taste; moisten to the height of the shellfish with half white wine and half water.

Let them cook with a lid on a high fire for ten minutes. Take them off the fire when the crayfish are red and let them cool in their *court bouillon*.

When you are ready to serve, lay the crayfish on a dish.

MUSSELS MARINIERE

MOULES MARINIERES

Take some mussels from the Mediterranean. Wash
them, clean them thoroughly. For each two pounds of
mussels, opened and dry, take a handful of parsley,
three cloves of garlic chopped fine, three laurel leaves,
a clove, a tiny bit of nutmeg, a pinch of flour, two
spoons of fine olive oil and a glass of fresh water to
correct the very salt water of the mussels. Cook them
by sautéeing them; at the end add a little ground white
pepper.

2 lbs. mussels opened with a knife—not steamed—with $\frac{1}{2}$ cup
chopped parsley, $\frac{1}{2}$ tsp. flour, 3 Tbs. olive oil. Sauté. When
half-cooked add $\frac{3}{4}$ cup water.

FRIED POURPRILLONS

POURPRILLONS FRITS

Have a young octopus, wash it carefully without
beating it. Put in its cap a clove of garlic, stick a needle
through the body and turn the head down so that the
legs cover it.

Drop it slowly into boiling oil to cover it completely.
The flesh of the octopus will shrivel up like a mushroom. Then let it cook on a tiny fire in a pan with
some oil, fifty grams of capers, fifty grams of sliced
black olives. Pepper and salt if the olives are not
salted.

When the oil is reduced and capers and olives melted,
pour this sauce, strained, over the octopus.

2 heaping Tbs. each of capers and sliced olives.

MUSSELS MARINIERE

MOULES MARINIERES

Have some very fat mussels from Calais or the Mediterranean. Wash them, brush them, clean them seriously by rinsing them in several waters. Put them in a very large wrought-iron saucepan with a laurel leaf, and one large onion, cut in slices, per two pounds of mussels. Open them by sautéeing them without covering the saucepan.

If the liquid is clean, keep half of it; if it is muddy, throw it away. Then, add three quarters of a glass of rather dry wine and a good nut of butter per two pounds of mussels, and let them sauté on a big wood fire. At the end add some chopped parsley with a little garlic.

When you serve add some white pepper just ground.

With mussels from Calais, it is sometimes necessary to add coarse salt (not fine salt); with those from the Mediterranean it is better to throw away the water which is extremely salty and to replace it with clear water.

For each 2 lbs. mussels: $^2/_3$ cup white wine, 2 Tbs. butter.   Ocean mussels do need a little salt.

MUSSELS ON SKEWERS

MOULES EN BROCHETTE

Have some very fat mussels, clean them carefully and open them in a saucepan on the fire.

When they are opened, take them off the fire, take them out of their shells, wash them in water to remove the sand, dry them on a white cloth.

On little skewers thread a mussel, a piece of *bacon* of the same size, and so on, taking care not to squeeze the mussels and the *bacon* too tight so that the liquid can penetrate well.

Put the skewers on charcoal and grill them, turning them over.

When the fat is cooked the mussels ought to be also, without being dried up.

Take the skewers off the fire, arrange them as they are on a dish, pour over them some melted butter worked with chopped parsley and seasoned with salt, pepper, and the juice of a lemon.

One can also dip the mussels in oil and roll them in bread crumbs before skewering them.

BURGUNDIAN SNAILS

ESCARGOTS A LA BOURGUIGNONNE

Have some vine snails and let them fast for several days. Wash them in several waters, lightly salted and vinegared. Cook them in boiling water with salt, pepper and a *bouquet garni,* for about half an hour. Take the snails out of the shell and remove the black part. Throw them into a basin of warm water, wash them and drain them. Clean and wash the shells carefully, turn them upside down on a plank and let them dry well.

Prepare the "frâa," that is a paste made with butter, the crumbs of stale bread passed through a sieve, garlic, and parsley both chopped very fine; salt; pepper; work the paste well with a fork, put back a snail into each shell and fill the orifice with a large nut of "frâa."

Garnish a rimmed dish with the shells, open-side up, and put in a very hot oven for a few minutes.

Serve boiling hot. The breadcrumb in the "frâa" is optional; it absorbs the excess of butter and, when lightly browned, tastes well, but the bread must be made with good wheat otherwise do not use it.

Canned snails are useable. Follow directions on tin for preliminary preparation. "Frâa" for 1 doz. snails: $1/_4$ lb. butter, $1/_3$ cup bread crumbs, 3 cloves crushed garlic, $1/_3$ cup finely minced garlic.

SNAILS A L'ARLATENQUE

LIMACES A L'ARLATENQUE

Have one hundred and fifty snails or two hundred *mourguettes*, that is small white snails striped with black.

Let them marinate for a quarter of an hour in some very good highly salted vinegar. Stir for a long time, then wash in a lot of water. Scrape the bottom end of the shells, then put them to steep in clear water until the snails come out of the shell.

Plunge them in cold water, put them on the fire, and at the first boil, change the water. Put the snails in the shells.

Add laurel, fennel, orange peel, a few grains of coriander, four cloves and let cook for two to two and a half hours according to whether they are snails or *mourguettes*.

Prepare a sauce with half a glass of olive oil, two nice sliced anchovies, fifty grams of onion chopped fine, one hundred and fifty grams of tomato or purée, two spoons of capers, garlic, parsley, pepper and salt. *Bind* with

some flour and brown lightly. Brown the snails for
ten minutes, add a little bouillon to have a thick sauce,
let it simmer for an hour on a small fire. Serve and eat
the snails "à la sucuello," that is sucking them in
through the orifice.

One can add to this sauce either hazelnuts or pounded
almonds.

POUTARDE

Toward July, when the gray mullet, coming from
the Mediterranean return to the estuaries to swim up
to lay their eggs in fresh water, and are full of roe—
open them through the belly and take out the strings
of roe, taking care to let them adhere unbroken to a
piece of flesh; on an average one gathers a pound of roe
per gray mullet weighing three to five pounds.

Let them steep for forty-eight hours in salted water;
then, scrape them with a small spoon and remove the
filaments of blood.

Next lay the strings of roe between two very clean
white wood planks, and first put on top a light weight
to flatten them out, then progressively increase the
weight so that, without being crushed, the strings of roe
become as flat as sole.

This done, by the piece of flesh adhering to the string,
hang these flat cakes of roe in the hot sun and a strong
mistral. Let them dry; thus you will have poutarde,
which is eaten with bread like chocolate and which, by
its special taste of fermented fish, pleases connoisseurs,
although its flavor is less subtle than that of caviar.

Menu

ABOUT CERTAIN GAME
OF FUR
AND FEATHER

DE QUELQUES GIBIERS DE POIL ET DE PLUME

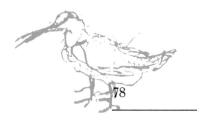

WOODCOCK WITH PORT

BECASSE AU PORTO

Having autumn and winter woodcock which have spent some time in our region—not migratory woodcock from the seaside, which are often detestable and taste fishy—let them hang by the beak in the pantry for from ten to thirty days, according to the temperature; woodcock demands to be eaten when it is very high—fresh woodcock just do not exist.

Proceed as for snipe; but one needs a meat press and one adds port and old cognac.

ROAST SNIPE

BECASSINES ROTIES

Having killed some September snipe, eat them quite fresh when you come back from the shoot. Pluck but do not empty them, push one or two peppercorns into the anus, surround them with a thin slice of *bacon*, and put them on spit in front of a light wood fire.

Under the birds to be roasted, lay slices of stale bread, two fingers' thick, and well buttered. Baste during the cooking with the gravy which drips into the roasting pan.

Ten minutes of a brisk fire should be enough to roast the snipe. The flesh should stay bloody.

Take them off the spit, arrange them on a silver or pewter dish. On a chafing dish place the slices of bread, cut the snipe quickly into four portions, mash the entrails onto the bread, press the carcasses, baste with the liquid from the carving and roasting, moisten with a small glass of cognac. Add salt, and pepper; let the bread slices flare slightly, then arrange the portions of snipe and the heads together with some grilled bacon slices.

Serve very hot on boiling hot plates.

Another method, more simple, is for each guest himself to carry out the process of fixing his own bread slice over a chafing dish, but without flaring it in cognac —by so doing he will be served better and quicker and to his own taste.

POACHED PARTRIDGE

PERDREAU POCHE

Take a partridge, pluck it, dress it, stuff the inside with *foie gras*, either of goose or duck, and a truffle cut into large pieces—if you have neither, use a truffled pig's trotter. Salt and pepper heavily with ordinary pepper, and scatter a few peppercorns of white and aromatic pepper here and there.

Sew up the belly; wrap the partridge in a paper-thin slice of *lard*; tie it up, or better still, swaddle it in a piece of muslin, taking good care to leave a string by which to hang it up.

This done, put some water and peppercorns into a pot without a lid, bring it to a brisk boil, then drop in the partridge, which will make the water stop boiling, and leave it hanging in the water by its string attached to a rod placed across the pot.

When the water begins to boil again, count twenty to twenty-five minutes for the bird to be cooked.

Unswaddle the partridge and serve it as it is; the flesh should just be done, should be rare, and from the inside of the carcass a delicate aroma of *foie gras* and truffles should emerge.

This recipe can also be used for pheasant which must have at least an hour's cooking.

THRUSHES THE ARDENNES WAY

GRIVES ARDENNAISES

Take six or a dozen thrushes of the autumn migration, taken with a snare. Into a deep, round cooking pot or an earthenware sauté pan put a nut of butter, some pieces of *unsmoked bacon*, cut into pieces about the length and thickness of a little finger, and the thrushes, well plucked but not drawn.

Add a few leaves of fresh sage, salt and pepper, cover and let them cook gently for at least an hour.

Serve in the pan in which they were cooked.

QUAILS IN ASHES

CAILLES DANS LA CENDRE

At the end of September, beginning of October, after you have killed some fat quail, pluck and empty them. Next roll them, duly salted and peppered, each separately, in a well-buttered vine leaf; tie them and bury them in the very hot wood ash of the hearth.

When they are cooked, serve them on very hot plates.

Menu

THRUSHES WITH JUNIPER

GRIVES AU GENIEVRE

Take six or twelve thrushes. Pluck them, draw them, stuff their insides with juniper mixed with a few peppercorns. Sew up the bellies, wrap the birds up in a thin slice of *pork lard*, and tie them up.

Into a sauté pan or a cocotte, put some *bacon* cut into pieces of two fingers' width by half a finger long and thick, and let them cook without a lid on a gentle fire. At the end add a small glass of genièvre gin and croutons previously sautéed in butter.

Serve in the pan.

ROAST WOOD PIGEON

PALOMBE ROTIE

In October, at the time of migration, take a wood pigeon. Empty it, put in on a spit, *barded with bacon,* in front of a clean fire of vine cuttings and on top of some well toasted bread, cut lengthwise to have a little crust.

Baste the wood pigeon and the bread; do not let it overcook.

When it is done to a turn take the animal out. Set aside the wings and legs. Put the white meat and the inside of the bird onto a plate, add the brain and chop it all up.

When it is chopped very fine, dilute it with a little oil, add pepper, salt, nutmeg, fairly strongly. Grind it all up well and spread it on the roast.

Sprinkle with old eau-de-vie and set it on the grill or in the oven for three or four minutes without burning it.

Lay the wings and legs on top of the wood pigeon. Serve very hot.

The same recipe is used also in the Landes for woodcock.

WILD DUCK FROM CHAMPAGNE

CANARD SAUVAGE CHAMPENOIS

Cut your wild duck in pieces, set aside the liver. Brown the pieces of duck in butter. When they are a good golden color, sprinkle with flour and add a glass of very good red wine, a glass of bouillon and some mushrooms. Salt and pepper; add a *bouquet garni* and let it cook covered, on a low heat.

A quarter of an hour before serving, add the liver crushed in a little red wine and one or two spoonfuls of tomato purée; let it reduce and *bind*.

Pour the sauce over the pieces laid on a dish and surround them with croutons of bread in sautéed butter.

YOUNG WILD PIGEONS WITH OLIVES

RAMEREAUX AUX OLIVES

Table some young pigeons, empty them, and into the inside put a stuffing of beef, veal, sausage meat— seasoned with aromatic pepper—nutmeg, and sliced truffles. Tie them up and let the pigeons brown briskly in a heavy, shallow pan. Then, put into a saucepan *bacon*, shallot, onion, and make a light *roux* with flour. Add salt, pepper, a *bouquet garni*. Put in the pigeons, moisten with good bouillon. Let them simmer gently for just under an hour with the saucepan covered. In the last twenty minutes add some pitted green olives which have been well desalted and a glass of cognac. Let them braise well and reduce.

Serve the birds on a dish surrounded by the olives and covered with the strained sauce which ought to be rich and thick.

A nice way to do even tame pigeon. For stuffing, allow $1/3$ lb. mixed meat per bird. Cook each bird with 1 Tbs. butter, 2 Tbs. small cubes bacon, 2 shallots, $1/2$ cup bouillon, 6 Tbs. cognac.

WILD DUCK WITH CARROTS AND OLIVES

CANARD SAUVAGE AUX CAROTTES ET AUX OLIVES

Empty the wild duck, mallard, coral beaks—called espagnols—large pintails, spoonbill ducks, not forgetting to remove the pocket of fat which is under the rump and which can have the taste of fish.

If you do not know whence the duck originates, let it brown briskly in processed lard, to let the rank grease, which may taste fishy, melt and throw it away.

Inside the duck put a stuffing, not too rich, made with the livers and shallot, finely chopped, stoned black olives which have been desalted, and season a little with white and aromatic pepper, nutmeg. Salt delicately. Sew up the belly and tie up the bird. In a large saucepan or cocotte, put butter, bacon fat, a few whole small onions, a shallot, a whole clove of garlic, a

tiny bit of flour, and make a light *roux*. Add salt,
pepper, nutmeg, fennel, thyme, laurel, parsley; make a
bed of round slices of young carrots (if the carrots are
old, blanch them); lay on the duck and moisten with
good bouillon.

Let it simmer gently, covered at least an hour and a
half; then in the last twenty minutes, add a glass of old
cognac, and pitted green olives which have been well
desalted. Arrange the duck on a dish surrounded with
the carrots and olives, the whole bathed in the strained
sauce which should be thick.

RAGOUT OF SCOTER DUCK

SALMIS DE MACREUSE

After a heavy shoot of scoter ducks (which are called
by different names in various regions of France, such
as coot, *judelles*, bléries), choose from among them some
young ones. Skin them while quite fresh. Cut them
up, retaining only the legs, the wings, and the breast.
Set aside the livers.

Into a deep round pot put butter, onion, crushed
garlic, and shallot; make a *roux* and let the pieces
brown. Sprinkle with flour, add some chopped *lard* or
bacon and the crushed livers, moisten with equal parts
of red wine and water, season with thyme, laurel,
parsley, aromatic and white pepper, salt, and add a
glass of cognac.

Let it simmer on a low fire.

One can make pâtés, as with hare, from the scoter
ducks, but only take the fillets of meat from the breast.

FILLET OF HERONS

FILET DE HERONS

Having killed some gray herons, pluck them, skin them, and from each bird take out the two nice fillets of meat which are to be found on the breast. The rest of the heron is only nerves and bones.

Either roasted or in a game ragout, the breast of gray heron yields nothing in delicacy and savor to that of wild duck.

This recipe from the Somme can also be used for the purple herons of the Camargue, which are still more delicate in taste.

PARTRIDGE WITH CABBAGE

PERDRIX AUX CHOUX

Take an old partridge and at least two tender young partridges. Pluck them, dress them and let them roast to a turn before a wood fire. Set them aside.

Cut some white cabbages lengthwise, blanch them with salt, and drain them.

In an earthenware pot put butter and *processed lard*, an onion, a small piece of *salt pork*; let it brown lightly; add the cabbage and the old partridge, and moisten with good bouillon and a finger of white wine; add peppercorns; and let it simmer for a good two hours at least. Add raw ham, cervelet, unsmoked Frankfort or Toulouse sausage, previously browned in butter, and the two young partridges; and let them simmer again for two or three hours, just moistening with bouillon if necessary.

Make a bed of cabbage on a dish while taking out the bones of the partridge, now completely broken up into pieces. Arrange the two young partridges with the rounds of sausage, ham, cervelet and the strained liquid, skimmed of fat, seasoned to taste with salt and freshly ground pepper.

LEG OF ROEBUCK OR SADDLE OF HARE

CUISSOT DE CHEVREUIL OU RABLE DE LIEVRE

Marinate for at least twenty-four hours with good red wine, a spoon of olive oil, salt, pepper, parsley, onions, shallots. Pour the marinade over from time to time. Lard it very thickly with strips of *bacon* and put it into the oven or on the spit with butter for at least two hours' cooking.

During this time boil the marinade for two hours, add the cooking liquid and some bouillon to which you have added a tablespoon of potato flour. When ready to serve add capers and a nut of fresh butter.

Wine to cover in small bowl. 400° oven. Sauce: $^1/_4$ cup bouillon for flour; finish with 2 Tbs. capers and 3 Tbs. butter stirred in off the fire.

FRICASSEE OF WILD RABBIT

LAPIN DE GARENNE EN GIBELOTTE

Skin and draw a wild rabbit, freshly killed; cut it in pieces, taking care to joint the bones without breaking them. In a deep round pot with butter, onions, and flour let the pieces of rabbit, the chopped liver, and the kidneys cook slightly and become golden. Add a *bouquet garni* while seasoning with thyme, salt, and black and white pepper. Moisten with a bottle of very good white wine from Bordeaux, Sauterne, Malromé, or Burgundy or Meursault. Cover and let simmer on a gentle fire. In the last half hour add some *bacon cubes* and mushrooms, previously lightly sautéed.

Arrange the pieces of rabbit with the mushrooms and the *bacon*; skim the fat off the sauce; salt and pepper to taste and encircle the dish with golden croutons sautéed in butter.

3 Tbs. butter, 2 onions, $^1/_4$ lb. *bacon* cubes, $^1/_2$ lb. mushrooms sautéed in butter.

WILD RABBIT AT REST, WITH OLIVES

LAPIN DE GARENNE AU GITE ET AUX OLIVES

Skin and draw a wild rabbit freshly killed. Brush the inside with English Savora mustard mixed with Colman's mustard and fill with a rich stuffing composed of beef, pork, sausage meat, and stoned black olives, chopped up with the liver and the kidneys; salt and season with thyme and white and aromatic pepper. Stick fine *lardoons* into the saddle and legs.

Sew up the belly; fold up the animal in such a way that it looks like a rabbit at rest; brush the outside with more Savora mustard; swaddle it in a thin piece of *lard* and tie it up.

Put it in an earthenware roasting pan to go into the oven for thirty-five minutes to three quarters of an hour, basting frequently, and add black and green olives which have been desalted and stoned.

Serve in the earthenware dish.

$^3/_4$ lb. stuffing of equal parts ground beef, pork, and sausage meat; add $^1/_4$ cup chopped olives. Use 450° oven.

LEG OF WILD BOAR
FROM THE FOREST OF ORLEANS IN LARD

CUISSOT DE SANGLIER DE LA FORÊT D'ORLEANS EN JAMBON

A large wild boar of three hundred pounds having been killed, cut off a leg weighing nineteen pounds, leave it out for three days in the winter air, then flay and skin it. Stick *lardoons* into the leg, cover it with its skin and a sheet of *lard*, put it into a big earthenware dish and let it bathe in a marinade made as follows:

In a saucepan put cut onion, sliced carrots, and shallots with butter or oil. Let them brown lightly; add salt, ordinary and aromatic pepper and red pepper, pimentos, cloves, thyme, sage, and laurel, half a bottle of very good dry white wine from Arbois or Burgundy, as much water again—and let it boil for a quarter of an hour. Pour this boiling marinated sauce over the leg

Menu

which for three days—as it has been said above—has been turned over and marinated.

On the morning of the day it will be eaten for luncheon, at 6:30 A.M. for lunch at 12:30 P.M.—which allows a quarter of an hour cooking time per pound— put the leg into a terrine to go on the fire, the leg well wrapped up in a white cloth and tied up very tight.

Moisten to the height of the leg with a bottle of good white wine, adding water and two or three glasses of concentrated bouillon. Add salt, pepper, thyme, clove, laurel, paprika, parsley, a *bouquet garni*, and sage and let it cook on a low fire.

Unwrap your leg and serve it with apples cut into rounds which have been cooked in butter in the dripping pan and with sliced fried potatoes accompanied either by a béarnaise sauce, or with a brown sauce made with the residue of the cooking liquid and seasoned with a dash of Worcestershire sauce.

STEWED MARMOTS

CIVET DE MARMOTTES

Having killed some marmots sunning themselves belly up in the sun with their noses in the air one sunrise in September, skin them and carefully put aside the mass of fat which is excellent for rubbing into the bellies of pregnant women, into the knees, ankles, and painful joints of sprains, and into the leather of shoes.

Cut up the marmot and treat it like stewed hare which has a perfume that is unique and wild.

SQUIRRELS

ÉCUREUILS

Having killed some squirrels in autumn, skin them the same day and empty them. Roll them up in a piece of *lard* and let them brown with some good quality butter in a copper saucepan. When they are a good golden color, salt them, cover, and let them cook on a very gentle fire.

One must use no spice of any kind which might entail the risk of taking away from the animal its exquisite nutty flavor.

ABOUT CERTAIN
DOMESTIC ANIMALS

DE QUELQUES ANIMAUX DOMESTIQUES

BEEF STEW

BŒUF MIROTON

Take what remains of the beef boiled in the pot-au-feu. Cut it in slices about half a finger long and two fingers wide.

In a lightly buttered earthenware dish, arrange the pieces of beef; salt; pepper; pour over them the miroton sauce as is mentioned in the chapter on sauces, sprinkle with some bread crumbs worked with chopped parsley and dot with butter.

Put in the oven to crisp. Serve in the dish.

This ancient recipe is fast disappearing. Once upon a time the concierges took upon themselves the task of filling a whole house with the smell of onions.

BEEF FROM THE POT-AU-FEU

LE BŒUF DU POT-AU-FEU

The bouillon having been made and served (as is explained in the chapter about soups), serve it with coarse salt and a garnish of carrots, turnips, potatoes, white cabbage, and leeks. Add the choice pieces of meat—the short ribs or bottom round—these parts boil down less and are fatter than the end of the sirloin or the neck, which have a tendency to become stringy.

In addition, to accompany the dish of beef, serve from chafing dishes:

A dish of the marrow bones to spread on pieces of bread

A dish of stuffed mushrooms

A dish of glazed onions

MENU

A dish of stuffed tomatoes or eggplant (aubergines)
A dish of pork, or long sausages, cooked with potatoes.

When understood thus the pot-au-feu constitutes by itself an excellent dinner for a family or shooting party.

The pot-au-feu becomes inedible, and loses its reputation, if one is led to follow the absurd methods of certain people in country or town who use no salt, throw away the first water of the meat bouillon, and so obtain nothing but leathery meat and a tasteless soup.

STEWED VEAL

BLANQUETTE DE VEAU

Take some breast of veal and cut it in pieces. Put the pieces into a saucepan and moisten them to the height of the meat with hot water. Add three or four onions, salt, pepper, a *bouquet garni*. Let it cook gently.

Halfway through the cooking, take out the meat, strain the bouillon.

In another saucepan melt some butter—a piece about the size of an egg; mix in two or three spoons of flour, let it cook for a few minutes until it becomes an ivory color; add the bouillon from the veal little by little. Let it cook for a quarter of an hour, then add the veal and half a pound of mushrooms.

Let it simmer on a low heat.

When you are about to serve arrange the meat on a dish. *Bind* the sauce with three or four yolks of egg, salt; pepper to taste; pour it over your meat.

This dish should look pale ivory; 3 lbs. veal, 3 Tbs. butter. Cook 1 hr. in water, 1 hr. in sauce.

BEEF A LA MALROME

BŒUF A LA MALROME

Take some beef, a piece of rump, and cut it in squares about the thickness of two fingers.

Let these pieces brown with some fat. Into a *roux* put onion, garlic, shallots, carrots, turnips, vegetables and let them cook slightly. Then put the beef into an earthenware pot which can go into the oven. Add salt, pepper, and cloves, and moisten to the height of the contents with red Malromé wine (a very good red Bordeaux). Cover with a lid and let it reduce on low fire for five or six hours. This done, take the reduced liquid, strain it and *bind* it while adding the necessary seasoning; nutmeg, parsley fine chopped; then pour it over the beef.

Same recipe for fillets of buck, venison, and wild boar.

5 lbs. rump: *roux*: 4 tsp. butter and 2 Tbs. flour. Then 2 large onions, 6 cloves garlic, 3 heads shallot, 1½ lbs. carrots, 2 white or purple turnips—in pieces—and extra vegetables to taste. Cover bottom of pot with vegetables; add beef and wine. Beef is served in strained sauce without vegetables.

BRAISED BEEF FROM DAUPHINE

BŒUF EN DAUBE DU DAUPHINE

Arrange slices of *lard* in an earthenware pot. Add the beef, the pigs' trotters, the calf's trotter, the rinds, the carrots, a tomato and an onion stuck with cloves, a *bouquet garni*, salt, peppercorns and ground pepper, and some tomato consommé.

Add an ox tongue or a calf's head or a chicken; if you use the last, put it in only for the time necessary for it to cook.

Moisten the whole with red and white wine.

Let it cook for at least twelve hours.

An hour before serving, skim the fat carefully, add a little Liebig's essence or *meat glaze* and a good wine glass of cognac. Above all no water.

For ten people : One must have : four pigs' trotters, a calf's trotter, 12 packets of rinds, 2 kilos of carrots, a tomato and an onion stuffed and stuck with cloves, an ox tongue or a calf's head, or a chicken, a pound of tomato consommé, a half quarter of a pound of *meat glaze* or Liebig's essence, three bottles of red wine, a bottle of white wine, a glass of cognac, two kilos of rump—a piece rather on the lean side.

For ten people: 2 large pieces of *bacon* or ham rind, 4$^1/_2$ lbs. carrots, 1 cup tomato juice and 1 cup beef broth (instead of tomato consommé), $^1/_2$ cup cognac, 5 lbs. lean rump. Cook at least heat.

VEAL MARENGO

VEAU MARENGO

Take some pieces of real veal, that is to say veal which cannot be baptized as sucking calf or bull, nor heifer or ox, veal which is still in the chrysalis period.

In a saucepan heat half oil, half butter. Brown the pieces of veal on a very brisk fire. Season with salt and pepper and sprinkle with flour. When the pieces of veal are nicely golden, put in three or five onions according to their size and chopped; two shallots, and a whole clove of garlic; a *bouquet garni*; and let it brown for ten minutes.

Moisten with a very good white Bordeaux.

When the wine is reduced, add one or two glasses of good bouillon or *meat glaze*.

Cover the saucepan and set it on the corner of the stove, letting it simmer on a gentle fire for at least two hours. Barely moisten if necessary with some bouillon.

A quarter of an hour before serving, take out the garlic, the shallot, the *bouquet garni*, add a pinch of red pepper and aromatic pepper and a few spoons of tomato sauce.

Let it simmer for a quarter of an hour to twenty minutes; previously you will have added some veal sweetbreads, veal kidneys which have been cut up, chipolatas—little sausages—which have already been cooked slightly.

Arrange the pieces of veal on a dish, crowned with the other ingredients, and golden croutons sautéed with butter alternating with fried eggs.

A good stew even without the accessories. 3 lbs. veal in 2 Tbs. each oil and butter. The 1 cup wine with $^3/_4$ cup bouillon, or 2 Tbs. *meat glaze* with $1^1/_2$ cup wine. 1 tsp. tomato paste, 2 Tbs. crushed tomato pulp substitute for tomato sauce.

VEAL WITH WHITE BURGUNDY

VEAU AU VIN BLANC DE BOURGOGNE

Put into a deep round pot some dry white Burgundy with a little water, a *bouquet garni*, garlic, salt, pepper.

Let it boil, plunge the pieces of veal into the pot and cook a little. Take out the pieces of veal, put into the pot some butter worked with flour and let it cook while stirring.

Menu

Pass the sauce through a sieve, then put it back with the pieces of veal and let it simmer gently.

Serve very hot.

Simmer 2 lb. veal cubes 20 min. in 1 cup wine and $1/4$ cup water. Then cook 2 hrs. after adding 3 Tbs. butter with 1 Tb. flour.

CALF'S LIVER WITH PRUNES

FOIE DE VEAU AUX PRUNEAUX

In a round earthenware pot make a *roux* with butter and flour, prepared with great care for half an hour and well darkened. Put in a whole calf's liver, stuck with strips of *lard*.

When the liver is lightly browned, moisten with warm water, add salt, pepper, onions, whole shallots, a *bouquet garni*, laurel leaf, thyme or savory, leaving out garlic and clove. Bring to a boil; then cover the pot and let the contents simmer for at least two hours and a half.

In the last half hour add twenty-five pitted prunes previously cooked in hot red wine, and a good glass of cognac.

Put the covered pot into the oven and let it go on cooking gently and reducing for an hour—you will have a rich and thick sauce.

On a white or plain-colored dish serve the meat over which you have poured the sauce and encircle it with the prunes.

Butcher should skin and lard liver. *Roux* : 4 Tbs. butter, 2 Tbs. flour. Attention: allow prunes to soak in 1 cup wine and $1/3$ cup cognac for several hours or simmer $1/2$ hour.

CALF'S LIVER WITH THREE SLABS

FOIE DE VEAU AUX TROIS TRANCHES

Cut some slabs of bread as large as a hand, one centimeter thick. Butter them lavishly and sprinkle them with pounded juniper berries. On each of them put a slice of calf's liver of the same size; salt; pepper; sprinkle with juniper.

On top of the veal put a thin slice of *bacon*, sprinkle again with juniper and pepper.

Arrange the slices in an earthenware dish, put it into a very brisk oven for about fifteen to twenty minutes, taking good care that the liver remains slightly rare to be creamy and melting.

Serve hot on the dish.

Use slices ¹/₄ inch thick of bread and liver.

MOCK RABBIT PATE

PATE DE LAPIN ARTIFICIEL

For 10 people: Take four or five scallops of veal of the size of the terrine, lean and flat and of about eight hundred grams and let them marinate for twelve hours in a good white Bordeaux with salt, pepper, spices, nutmeg, a *bouquet garni*, onions, shallots, and sliced carrots.

In a terrine about twenty-five centimeters long, put a few cloves, three laurel leaves, sprigs of thyme, nutmeg, aromatic peppercorn. On this bed of spices press a sheet of *lard* large enough to envelop and cover the whole terrine. Make layers, one on top of the other, as follows:

On the sheet of *lard* at the bottom, lay flat a veal cutlet which has been cut into narrow strips—about five or six. Between the strips of veal lay a slice of raw Bayonne ham, a slice of lean *unsalted bacon*, a slice of lean pork; salt; pepper; spread a layer of sausage meat, worked with a very little onion and shallot chopped fine, and scrapings of truffle.

Then start again the beds of veal, of raw ham, etc., putting here and there two or three truffles cut into large pieces, until terrine is full.

Push the meat down and fold the sheet of *lard* over to seal it; then, between the terrine at the side and the *lard*, push in some cloves and laurel leaves; on top of the *lard* casing lay a sliced onion, shallots, laurel leaf, a sprig of thyme, and aromatic peppercorns. Cover with a greased paper and close hermetically with the terrine lid. Let cook on a very gentle heat.

$3^1/_2$ lbs. veal. Bordeaux to cover. 10 inch long terrine.

WHOLE SHEEP ROASTED OUT OF DOORS

MOUTON ENTIER ROTI EN PLEIN AIR

Dig a hole one meter fifty by one meter and one meter deep. At the bottom lay a bed of flat stones and for three hours make a large fire so that you have a huge bed of embers—do not let smoke overshoot the hole by fifty centimeters.

On each side of the hole plant a big branch of green wood cut into a Y, letting a few branches overlap beneath the Y to act as hooks. Have a very long solid branch of oak or holly, on which you will thread a pretty sheep of about eighteen months or two years. Anchor the sheep solidly with wire or a noose onto its skewer, extend the legs with stakes of wood in such a way that nothing will move when the sheep is being turned above the fire.

Let it roast over very hot cinders for an hour and a half to two hours and have two or three large poles holding little bags filled with beef dripping to baste the sheep and prevent its burning. If you have no dripping use a bucket of oil or liquid fat and a brush made of heather or birch tied to the end of a stick. During the cooking throw on a full handful of coarse gray salt and a little pepper.

Remove the sheep from its skewer onto a bed made of green pine branches; hand round choice crackling morsels such as the ends of the ribs and the kidneys, rare tidbits unknown to people who are used to eating shut up in houses. It will be a positive revelation to them.

IRISH BOILED LEG OF MUTTON

GIGOT DE MOUTON BOUILLI IRLANDAIS

Into a large earthenware pot put some water; salt; pepper heavily. Add a lot of turnips and carrots cut into rounds and let them boil for a good half hour.

Menu

———————◇———————

Plunge the leg of mutton into the boiling water and let it boil over high heat, allowing a quarter of an hour per pound of meat.

Separately cook in water or steam some whole peeled potatoes. Serve the leg of mutton surrounded by potatoes and accompanied by a white sauce with capers and peppermint, that is to say a sauce made of flour, butter, moistened with bouillon, bound with an egg yolk and flavored to taste with capers, salt, pepper, and peppermint.

Enough water to cover. 3 lbs. each turnips and carrots. Sauce: 4 Tbs. butter, 2 Tbs. flour; cook slowly, add 2 cups cooking broth; thicken.

LEG OF LAMB EN COCOTTE OF AUVERGNE

GIGOT EN COCOTTE D'AUVERGNE

In an iron or cast-iron deep round or oval pot lined with enamel, put a pound of butter, carefully greasing the whole inside. Take some flat onions, all of the same size, and arrange them on the bottom of the pan. The onions must be six centimeters in diameter. Add thyme, laurel, a *bouquet garni*, chives, a mignonette, shallots—above all no garlic—salt, and peppercorns. On top lay the whole leg, taking care to fold back the shank so that the leg can fit into the pot. Sprinkle it with coarse salt and make some deep incisions with a knife. Butter it carefully and put it to cook on a small wood fire, if possible, allowing for a minimum of cooking time of a quarter of an hour per pound. From time to time lift the lid to see how the cooking is getting on.

Turn the leg over and add a little butter at the bottom if the onions are beginning to stick too much, because they must not burn.

In the last hour put some potatoes in to cook before the leg has finished cooking. Now add a glass of white wine. After a simmering of two to three hours according to the size of the leg, serve it all very hot. At the bottom of the pot you find a mixture of onions and potatoes which is delicious.

About $^1/_2$ cup wine. Mignonette: cracked white pepper, nutmeg, ginger, and clove.

SHEEP'S TROTTERS A LA POULETTE

PIEDS DE MOUTON A LA POULETTE

Singe them, scald them, clean them if the butcher has not done so.

Let them cook in a blanc, that is to say: in a saucepan put two to three liters of water, a few spoons of flour, two whole onions stuck with cloves, three carrots, a *bouquet garni*, salt, peppercorns, and the juice of a lemon. Bring to a boil, then add the trotters, let them cook half uncovered, skimming from time to time, three or four hours.

One can see that the feet are cooked when the middle bone detaches itself. Take the trotters out of the broth, drain them on a white cloth. Strain and reduce the broth.

In another saucepan make a light *roux* with butter and flour, add the reduced broth, some bouillon and bring to a boil. Add mushrooms, warmed in melted butter and chopped; *bind* with three egg yolks; add a handful of blanched and chopped parsley; add the juice of a lemon.   Throw the trotters into this sauce.

12 trotters boiled in 2-3 qts. water.   Sauce: for the *roux* use 3 Tbs. butter, 2 Tbs. flour, add 6 cups cooking liquid reduced to 3; $^1/_2$ lb. mushrooms in 2 Tbs. butter.

SAUSAGES WITH APPLES

SAUCISSES AUX POMMES

Take some beautiful apples, on the green side and cut them in rounds of no more than a tenth of a centimeter thickness.   Take out the pips.

In a cooking pan put a nut of butter and let some long sausages cook—they should have been previously pricked.   Then throw in the rounds of apple and let them brown.   Pepper only.

Serve the sausages on the bed of apples.

One apple in $^1/_4$ inch thick slices for each spiced 6 inch pork sausage.

SHEEPSFEET AND PACKETS

PIEDS ET PAQUETS

For about twelve people: Have six sheep's tripe, twelve sheep's feet, two calves' feet, three hundred to four hundred grams of veal hock.   Wash, brush, scrape, and dip into boiling water.

Prepare a chopped mixture of garlic and parsley (five cloves of garlic, a handful of parsley) and cut some *salt pork* into strips.

To make the packets, cut the tripe in squares (twenty centimeters by twenty centimeters); spread them with the chopped mixture, add salt and pepper and then, one by one, the pieces of *salt pork*. Close each packet with a skewer.

When you are going to put it on the stove, place a plate upside down at the bottom of a tall earthenware pot, cover it with a few slices of *lard*.

Prepare some chopped and strained tomatoes.

Put into the pot one by one: a round of packets, a row of tomatoes, and a row of feet until they are used up.

Add half a bottle of white wine, two laurel leaves, two or three crushed cloves of garlic, a carrot and sliced onion.

Let it cook on a low fire for from fifteen to eighteen hours. Strain, skim the fat off the sauce which you pour over the feet.

**Packets are rolled up squares of tripe. Use in 8 inch squares.
³/₄ lb. veal neck. 4 lbs. tomatoes.**

TRIPE A LA LYONNAISE

TRIPES A LA LYONNAISE

Take three sheep's tripe, two calves' feet, six sheep's trotters, cut them in pieces.

Take some small onions, carrots and a good two pounds of tomatoes. Have at hand some garlic, milled pepper and corns, two laurel leaves.

At the bottom of a tall earthenware stewpot put two plates side by side. Arrange successively; a row of

MENU

tripe, a row of onions, one of the feet and carrots, a row of tomatoes, three to four cloves of garlic, salt, pepper-corns, laurel. Add a large glass and a half of dry white wine. Let it cook on a gentle heat for twelve hours. Skim the fat before serving.

Knuckles and trotters with meat, 2 lbs. peeled whole onions, 3-4 carrots, $2^1/_4$ lbs. tomatoes peeled and chopped, $1^1/_4$ cups wine.

TRIPE WITH CIDER

TRIPES AU CIDRE

Take three sheep's tripe, two calves' feet. Clean them carefully and cut them in pieces. In a round iron casserole or earthenware pot put onions, carrots, sliced shallots, laurel leaf, a *bouquet garni*, pepper, salt, a crushed clove of garlic, a nut of butter and let it all cook slightly. Add the tripe and the feet and moisten with good cider. Let it simmer for six to eight hours. Take the fat off before serving.

3 large onions, 6 carrots, 6 shallots, 3 Tbs. butter, 1 qt. fresh or hard cider (if unavailable, use 1 qt. apple juice, $^1/_4$ cup calvados, juice one lemon).

PORK CHOPS WITH PIQUANT SAUCE

COTELETTES DE PORC A LA SAUCE PIQUANTE

In a round pot sauté slightly some pork chops with *processed lard* or butter. Set them aside when they are golden. Make a brown *roux*, at the last moment add a small handful of shallots sliced very fine, then some hot water, while stirring with a wooden spoon.

Pour in another half a glass of white dry Burgundy or a spoonful of wine vinegar.

Let it cook and reduce and strain the sauce when you have taken the fat off. Lastly put in the chops and let them simmer without a lid. At the final moment add some rounds of *cornichon*.

Serve very hot.

Make sauce ahead: 2 Tbs. butter, 1 Tbs. flour, 5-6 shallots, $^3/_4$ cup water—2 Tbs. wine or 1 Tbs. vinegar. 4 large chops. Cook chops in sauce $^1/_2$ hour.

ROAST TURKEY FOR A SHOOTING LUNCH

DINDON ROTI POUR DEJEUNER DE CHASSE

Have a fine farm turkey, pluck it and dress it. Stuff the inside with a stuffing of beef, veal, sausage meat, two or three red boudin (soft blood sausages) lightly grilled and chopped, and mashed roast chestnuts. Salt, flavor with pepper and spices, sew up the belly and tie the animal up with string.

Lay the turkey on an earthenware dish, dot with butter and put it in a gentle oven, basting frequently.

Serve the turkey on the earthenware dish accompanied by fried potatoes.

For a 14 lb. turkey use 1 lb. each ground beef, veal, and sausage meat and $^1/_2$ lb. chestnuts. If no boudin (blood sausage), chop turkey liver and 3 chicken livers, sautéed, plus $^1/_2$ lb. extra sausage meat.

PATE OF GOOSE OR DUCK WITH A CRUST

PATE EN CROUTE D'OIE OU DE CANARD

Having drawn and dressed a young goose or duck, cut the birds in pieces, taking care to joint it well and not to break the bones. Put the pieces in a dish and let them marinate for about ten hours with strong seasoning of salt, peppers, spices.

Make a lightly puffed pastry, and having left it to rest for ten hours or so, roll it out on a square, round, or oblong sheet of the thickness of half a finger.

Arrange the pieces of poultry and cover them with paste into the form of a dome.

Put into a hot oven, taking care to put the sheet on a brick so that it does not touch the bottom of the oven. Let it cook gently for at least a good hour. When the crust is a good golden brown, put on top, to finish off the cooking, a buttered paper so that the crust does not burn. Serve hot.

CASSOULET

Take some nice very white Soissons beans, let them soak in cold water for twelve hours, then cook them almost entirely (about two and a half to three hours).

Into a heavy and shallow straight-sided saucepan put some pieces of mutton and pieces of goose and let them brown until they are golden.

In a large stewpot brown some onions, shallots, cloves of garlic, a little chopped *bacon*; add a knuckle of veal, a calf's foot, smoked ham, raw sausages, salt, pepper, laurel. Put in the browned pieces of meat, the giblets of the goose, carcass, bones, etc.

Moisten with bouillon, add some spoons of tomatoes.

Let it reduce very slowly on a low heat (about two hours). This done, take a large earthenware dish which can go into the oven, cover the bottom with the beans, and over them the pieces of mutton, goose—add the goose neck stuffed with sausage meat, a truffled pig's foot and some slices of plain sausage which have been cooked. Pour the contents of the saucepan over, leaving aside the bones, the carcass, and the residue, and skimming the fat.

Put the filled dish into the oven to cook the beans and the meat again.

Have some bouillon or meat gravy to moisten if this is necessary. A quarter of an hour before serving sprinkle with bread crumbs worked with parsley, let it get golden brown, and serve hot in the dish.

First soak, then cook 3 lbs. beans. Sauté 3 lbs. boned lamb (6 lbs. shanks), 1 goose, boned and cut small. Then cook with 3 large onions, 6 shallots, 4 cloves garlic, $^1/_4$ lb. lard, $^1/_2$ or 1 veal knuckle with a little meat, $^1/_4$ lb. ham, a pound coarse pork sausages, $1^1/_2$ qts. bouillon, 2 Tbs. tomato paste.

PRESERVED GEESE OF THE LANGUEDOC

CONFITS D'OIES DU LANGUEDOC

Take four geese fattened to the point when they can no longer move about, cut them in four, removing wings and legs but leaving the skin. Set aside the fat livers. Scrape and remove all the fatty tissues and let them melt on a gentle heat in a large copper pan.

MENU

When the fat begins to boil drop in the carcasses, the wings and legs and let them cook until the fat has melted.

Take these pieces out, salt them, arrange them in big stoneware jars and pour over them the liquid fat, lightly salted.

You have in this way the preserve which can be kept for several months.

It can be eaten cold when it comes out of the pot, with no further preparation after the goose grease has been melted. But generally people prefer to serve it either with peas, or with a tomato sauce, or in a cassoulet, or with rice in stock, a second cooking being usually recommended.

For the record one should note that preserved goose is also used in the Midi in making an excellent cabbage soup. In the north it can be added to a good choucroute.

GALANTINE OF PRESERVED GOOSE

GALANTINE DE CONFITS D'OIE

Take the bones out of a goose fat enough to die of it. Cut the breast into slices, cut white veal and the goose liver into little tongue shapes; chop the remains of the goose flesh with truffles.

Arrange, lengthwise, in the skin which covers the wings and the breastbone, these little tongue shapes with three whole truffles, and sew up as in all galantines.

Let it just go through the oven and then put it to cook in a double boiler for two and a half hours—in a well-sealed terrine, or in a soldered can if you want to have a preserve.

With the skin of the goose's neck one can make a sausage in the same way by adding the bits and pieces of the goose flesh, truffles, veal, and sausage meat.

PATE DE FOIE GRAS WITH PORT

PATE DE FOIE GRAS AU PORTO

Take several fine specimens of foie gras (very fat and white goose liver), clean them carefully, taking out the veins, the fibers, and the green. Wash them in cold salted water and let them soak for a good hour. Dry them and put them on an earthenware dish surrounded by goose grease. Let them cook on a very gentle heat for ten minutes at most.

Take them out and, when the livers have got cold again, lay in a big terrine very thin slices of Arles sausage, the livers, some truffles, and continue in this way until the terrine is full. Pour over a very hot sauce of calf's foot, very highly seasoned with spices, to which has been added some old port. Let it get cold.

Unmold it so as to have a dish robed in jelly. Serve with red currant jelly.

HOW TO MAKE CHICKEN TENDER

POULETS A DEVENIR TENDRES

In order to make chickens immediately edible, take them out of the hen-run, pursue them into open country, and when you have made them run, kill them with a gun loaded with very small shot.

The meat of the chicken, gripped with fright, will become tender. This method used in the country of the Fangs (Gabon) seems infallible even for the oldest and toughest hens.

FRICASSEE OF CHICKEN

FRICASSEE DE POULET

Have a nice chicken and joint it.

In a cast-iron cooking pot, before a good wood fire, cook lightly some pieces of *bacon*. When they are nicely golden, take them out and lightly cook the pieces of chicken. Mix them all up and sprinkle with flour and generously with shallots finely chopped with parsley. Salt, pepper, and cover. Let it simmer slowly and for a long time on a gentle heat. Add a good glass of cognac half an hour before serving.

$^1/_4$ lb. *bacon*, 1 Tbs. flour, 5 shallots. Cook 2 hrs. Add $^1/_3$ cup cognac.

CHICKEN WITH ALMONDS

POULET AUX AMANDES

Take some nice chickens and cut them in pieces without breaking the bones. In a heavy and shallow straight-sided saucepan brown some cut onions, a dash of garlic and shallot; then the pieces of chicken so that they are a good golden color.

This done, pour the contents of the pan into a big saucepan, having strained the liquid so that the garlic and onion are removed. Put in the pieces of chicken, add butter, a finger of wine and of cognac, a *bouquet garni*, cloves, pepper, salt; just moisten with bouillon.

Add the chopped livers, pieces of ham cut fine, and cubes of raw bacon. Sprinkle with a little flour. Let it reduce and simmer until there is practically no more liquid.

Just before you serve make a sauce with four to six egg yolks to which cream has been added, and *bind* over a gentle fire or in a double boiler so that the sauce does not curdle. Add the juice of one lemon and in the sauce mix well some almonds and hazelnuts pounded into small pieces.

Arrange pieces of chicken at the bottom of a warm dish, cover it all with sauce, and garnish the dish with croutons well sautéed in butter.

2 broilers sautéed with 3 onions in 3 Tbs. butter. For simmering: add 2 Tbs. butter, 2 Tbs. each white wine and cognac, $^1/_2$ cup bouillon, $^1/_4$ lb. cubed ham, 2 Tbs. *bacon* cubes, and 1 Tbs. flour. For sauce: $1^1/_2$ cups heavy cream.

VALENCIAN ARROZ

ARROZ A LA VALENCIANA

Cook a large handful of string beans in water. When they are cooked, take them off the stove and keep the water in which they were cooked.

Strip the leaves off and carefully clean three artichokes and cut the hearts into four pieces. Peel two or

Menu

three large tomatoes and squeeze them to get the seeds out.

Open a half liter of cockles, a half liter of mussels and a liter of clams; keep the liquid from the shellfish.

Put some oil into a round cooking pot and brown well a chicken cut in pieces. When it is a good golden brown, take out the pieces and cook a large onion and a clove of garlic cut into very small pieces. Then throw in half a pound of rice well washed and dried, and three times the volume of the rice in a liquid made up of the cooking water from the beans, the liquid from the shellfish, and completed with water if necessary. Salt and pepper; put in the chicken, the mussels, the cockles, the clams, and the artichokes, stirring it so that it is all well mixed.

Let it cook on a low flame without touching it or covering it. When there is no more liquid it will all be done. You can add some sweet peppers according to your taste.

2 cups cockles, 2 cups mussels and 4 cups clams.

CHICKEN WITH RICE

POULE AU RIZ

Take a hen neither too young nor too old. Put it into a deep, round cooking pot and let it cook with butter until it is nicely golden, then take it out. In the pot, cook some onions chopped fine with a bouquet of laurel, shallots, pepper, and two tomatoes cut in pieces. When the whole is well cooked put the chicken back and moisten it with bouillon to the height of the bird. Add the rice, previously washed in cold water, salt to taste, and add, if you like, a tiny dash of saffron.

Let it cook two and a half hours with a lid on a slow flame.

3 Tbs. butter, 3 large onions; $^1/_2$ cup rice.

PRESSED DUCK

CANARD AU SANG

This dish must be made and eaten within two hours of the death of the duck at the time of the spring regattas. As the duck is killed by suffocation when its neck is wrung and the breast pressed, this process may, in stormy weather, cause the blood to curdle and so make the dish dangerously toxic.

Therefore, having suffocated a duck, dressed, and drawn it and laid aside the liver, let it roast lightly on a quick wood fire for between twenty to twenty-five minutes. Cut it up at the table, arranging on a platter to keep warm over a low burner, the breast, wings, and legs—which one will later reheat on the grill, because these last should be only barely cooked. In a meat press put the chopped liver and the carcass you have left; add a large glass of good red wine, and press.

In a metal dish over a burner collect the liquid made up of blood and wine, add a glass of cognac, let it flame, and finally add a good lump of butter, stirring all the time. When the butter is melted, season strongly with pepper and arrange the pieces of duck in the full boiling sauce. Serve on hot plates.

CHICKEN MARENGO

POULET MARENGO

Put in a saucepan some olive oil, a crushed clove of garlic; heat and brown pieces of chicken.

When these pieces are a good golden color, take them out and make a *roux* with a spoon of flour.

When the *roux* is well browned, moisten with good bouillon, put back the pieces of chicken, salt, and pepper, and let simmer on a low flame.

Half an hour before serving, add some sautéed mushrooms, a few spoons of tomato purée, and pitted olives. Just as you serve, sprinkle with croutons of bread fried in butter.

2 Tbs. oil, 1 Tbs. flour, 1 cup chicken stock; $1/_2$ lb. mushrooms sliced and heated in 2 Tbs. butter; 2 Tbs. tomato purée and $1/_4$ cup black olives.

COLD FRICASSEE OF CHICKEN

POULET EN FRICASSEE FROID

Have two nice chickens, cut them in pieces without breaking the bones. In a round cooking pot cook the pieces with butter until they are very golden. Salt and pepper; moisten with a dry white wine—Montlouis, Epernay, Meursault—and let them simmer covered for an hour and a half. At the last moment add a dash of garlic, tarragon, parsley, and chervil—all finely chopped—and pepper freshly ground.

Lay the pieces in a terrine or deep dish, pour over the gravy, chill, and let jell.

Serve cold at a hunting meal in the open air.

4 Tbs. butter, 1¹/₂ cups wine, 2 Tbs. chopped fresh tarragon or 1 tsp. dry.

CHICKENS WITH RICE

POULETS AU RIZ

Have one or two good chickens, cook them in the oven, well basted with butter and fat.

Having cooked some rice in the Indian way, very white and well dried, add half a coffee spoon of meat extract and saffron to which water has been added to give color, a large lump of butter, and the gravy from the chicken.

Heat up the rice, sprinkling it with grated Gruyère, Holland, and parmesan cheese. Serve the chickens on the bed of rice.

4 Tbs. butter with the fat from the chicken. Cook whole in 400° oven about 45 min. or until done. Steam ¹/₄ cup patna rice. 1¹/₂ Tbs. butter and 2 Tbs. cheese per person.

ABOUT CERTAIN VEGETABLES

DE QUELQUES LÉGUMES

A GREEN CHICKEN

POULE VERTE

Take a piece of ham, some *bacon*, some sausage meat of pork or veal, some soft bread crumbs, and parsley. Chop it all up; salt and pepper.

Blanch a kale, take out the heart; chop it, and mix it with the meats.

Mix it all up with two whole beaten eggs and half a glass of milk. Roll the stuffing up in several large kale leaves, laid one on top of the other in such a way as to give the appearance of a galantine of fowl.

Tie it up and put it to cook in boiling water with some fat, some potatoes—like a cabbage soup—for one and a half to two hours. Salt; pepper with aromatic and ordinary pepper.

Untie the green chicken and serve it surrounded by potatoes. The broth makes an excellent soup.

A large stuffed cabbage roll. Stuffing: $^1/_3$ lb. each ham, pork sausage, and pork or veal; $^1/_2$ cup bread crumbs, $^1/_2$ cup parsley leaves (use $^1/_4$ lb. *lard* only if sausage is very lean).

ARTICHOKES WITH OIL AND GARLIC

ARTICHAUTS A L'HUILE ET A L'AIL

Cut each of four artichokes into four pieces; take out the choke, fold back the leaves and let them steep for an hour in cold water.

In a deep pot or frying pan heat a large glass of olive oil at a brisk heat. When the oil is boiling throw the quarters of artichokes in and let them cook until the leaves are well fried. Salt; remove the pan to the side of the stove, cover, and let it simmer gently for an hour and a half.

Five minutes before serving, add chopped garlic and parsley; pepper it well, and serve the artichokes with what remains in the saucepan.

After frying artichokes in $^3/_4$ cup oil, simmer. Season by adding $^1/_4$ cup chopped parsley with 2 large cloves garlic and pepper, and by scraping the glaze from the bottom of the pan.

BELGIAN ENDIVE IN ITS JUICE

ENDIVES AU JUS

Take some nice Belgian endive which has been wash-ed, pared, and dried. Put a good lump of butter into a deep cooking pot and let it heat. Add the endive and let them cook just until they are golden brown.

Salt and pepper; cover the pot and let it simmer for at least an hour and a half without adding water.

In the last quarter of an hour, if you have too much liquid, let it reduce with the lid off.

This recipe can be used for turnips and Jerusalem archichokes.

$1^1/_2$ lbs. white medium-sized endives; at least 4 Tbs. butter.

GLAZED ONIONS

OIGNONS GLACES

Take some onions from our own Northern region, all the same size, at least six to ten centimeters, into which you will put a clove next to the root.

Arrange them tightly packed in an enameled earthenware dish on a light bed of butter; salt and pepper. Moisten with bouillon to the height of the onions.

Let it reduce on a gentle heat without a lid for at least two hours. On each onion lay a lump of sugar, sprinkle with granulated sugar, then put the dish in the oven to glaze the onions.

Serve when the liquid, which should have reduced, is caramelized.

Onions at least 2-3 inches in size.

VEGETABLE PRESERVE

CONFIT DE LEGUMES

Into a deep cooking pot put a large lump of butter, six onions cut in moon-shaped slices, a quarter of a pound of coarsely chopped lean *bacon*. Let them cook gently over a low fire but without letting them brown. When the onions and the *bacon* are slightly melted, dredge with a good spoon of flour and stir.

Next add three chicory, three lettuce (which have previously been blanched in salted boiling water, then thrown into cold water and finally have been well drained), then a *bouquet garni*, salt, white and aromatic pepper (both peppercorns and powder), and three leaves of laurel.

Cover and let it cook on a gentle heat for three hours at least, adding a few spoons of bouillon or *meat glaze* so that it does not stick to the pan. Lay on top, cut side up, six tomatoes, cut through the middle, seeded but not peeled.

Menu

Cover and let it reduce yet another good hour until the preserve seems very creamy.

To make the dish richer you can add pork sausages, long sausages, rounds of Toulouse sausages which have been lightly browned in butter; or, as in the Mareuil region in the Vendée, pigs' feet cooked in water, boned and recooked in the preserve.

4 Tbs. butter.

LEEKS IN RED WINE

POIREAUX AU VIN ROUGE

Peel a dozen or two leeks, leaving scarcely any green. Wash them, wipe them and dry them with a cloth.

Into the bottom of a saucepan put a pound and a half of *bacon* cut in pieces and arrange the leeks on top.

Moisten thoroughly with three quarters of red wine and a quarter of water. Above all don't blanch the leeks beforehand or else they will be soft. Add only salt, pepper, and cloves. Let them cook gently for at least two hours, having covered the saucepan with buttered paper. At the end of this time the leeks will be cooked, rosy, and firm and the liquid will be reduced.

Now in a long heat-proof dish arrange the leeks. Take some of the liquid which you will *bind* with an egg yolk. Garnish the dish all round and in the middle with rounds of Toulouse sausage previously lightly cooked and sprinkle all over with bread crumbs worked with parsley.

Let it brown and go on reducing in the oven so that the dish has a creamy appearance and the leeks don't swim about.

Do not add any onion, garlic, scallion, etc., but only ordinary and cayenne pepper; strengthen with cloves.

Use large leeks, 3 cups wine and 1 cup water. Use $^3/_4$ cup of skimmed cooking liquid for sauce. About $^1/_4$ cup bread crumbs and $^1/_4$ cup finely chopped parsley. 300° oven about 20 min.

GARNISHED SAUERKRAUT

CHOUCROUTE GARNIE

Use a pound of sauerkraut per head. Take some nice sauerkraut straight from the tub; wash it and drain carefully.

Into a cooking or earthenware pot put butter, place very good *processed lard* or goose fat, the sauerkraut, a piece of rump steak, and pork butt or even some preserved goose. Moisten to the height of the ingredients with some good bouillon. Add several juniper berries and a good pinch of peppercorns. Cover, and let simmer for three or four hours on a gentle heat, then add half a bottle of good Rhine or Epernay wine.

If the sauerkraut is to be served for lunch, begin it in the afternoon of the previous day—it can never be overcooked.

Two or three hours before serving add some whole round potatoes and, an hour before, Toulouse or Morteau sausage, Strasbourg and Frankfurt sausages, and cervelat.

Skim the fat before serving.

Per person: 2 Tbs. each of butter and other fat; $^1/_4$ lb. each beef and pork. 1 small piece goose, 3 new potatoes, $^1/_2$ cup wine, $^1/_4$ cup hard spicy sausage.

RED CABBAGE WITH CHESTNUTS

CHOU ROUGE AUX MARRONS

Choose a red cabbage of about two pounds, a fine and very tight head, and tie a piece of string firmly round it. Cut off a small round from the stump and hollow out the cabbage through the stump, leaving a thickness of the leaves of about five centimeters. Sprinkle the inside with salt and pepper.

Garnish the hole with a stuffing made up of one part meat--beef, veal, pork, mutton, or sausage—and the other part of boiled and chopped chestnuts. Work this stuffing well together, mix it with an egg *roux* and flavor the whole with salt, pepper, and spices.

Close the orifice with the round from the stump and two or three of the large outer leaves in the form of a shell.

Wrap the cabbage up in a large slice of *pork fat back* or *lard* and tie it carefully; for even greater ease of handling put it into a small-meshed net, by means of which it will be easy to turn and to remove from the saucepan.

In a separate saucepan or pot brown slightly some small pieces of meat, bones, *lean bacon* with onions and carrots, parsley, thyme, laurel, and what remains of the heart of the cabbage. When everything has been slightly cooked, place the cabbage in the pan, pour over it one or two large bottles of red Bordeaux and a good half liter of bouillon. Salt, pepper well, add two cloves, and put it on a very brisk flame.

After bringing it to a good boil, move the saucepan to the side of the fire, cover it and let it simmer for eight to ten hours, watching the cooking very carefully to moisten it slightly with bouillon if necessary.

An hour before serving, take out the cabbage, un-swaddle it, and put it aside on a very hot dish.

Take a little of the strained liquid and in a saucepan add two pounds of chestnuts, boiled, peeled and crushed, and let them simmer; then, in a third sauce-pan make a *roux* with a little flour; add the remainder of the strained liquid; *bind* with an egg yolk, salt, pepper, and season to taste with nutmeg.

Encircle the cabbage with chestnuts and pour the sauce over it. Divide it into slices like a melon.

Stuffed, braised, whole cabbage served with a purée and a sauce. Stuffing: 1 cup sausage or any mixture of well-spiced, fatty ground meat mixed with 1 cup cooked, chopped chestnuts and a *roux* made with 2 Tbs. butter, 2 Tbs. flour and having 2 egg yolks blended in. Braise: $^1/_2$ lb. meat, $^1/_2$ lb. *lard*, 2 large sliced carrots, 3 medium sliced onions, 2 cups bouillon, enough wine to cover. Purée: 1 cup cooking liquid, 2 lbs. chestnuts. Sauce: 2 Tbs. butter, 2 Tbs. flour.

INDIAN RICE

RIZ A L'INDIENNE

Take some good Indian or Carolina rice, wash it care-fully in a lot of cold water, frequently renewed.

Let a lot of water boil in a very large stewpot, and when the water is boiling fast throw in the rice and let it boil, vigorously stirring all the time.

When at about the end of a quarter of an hour or twenty minutes the rice is cooked—it ought to be nei-ther crisp nor soft—take it off the stove, throw it in a sieve to drain it. Then, quickly wash it in a lot of cold water two or three times under a tap, throwing it each time in a sieve.

MENU

To finish, plunge the rice back into very hot water, drain it in a sieve, put the sieve over the stewpot in which the water is still boiling and let the rice dry in the steam.

Serve hot, either with tomato sauce or curry sauce to go with a dish of veal, of chicken, etc.

FRIED POTATOES SOUFFLE
POMMES DE TERRE FRITES SOUFFLEES

Take some Dutch potatoes, very healthy and smooth without sprouts, a deep frying pan with its basket, and frying fat made up either of oil and fat of a beef kidney, or of *lard*, beef dripping and oil. Peel the potatoes and cut them up carefully in the form of perfect cubes; then in lengthwise slices of the cube of a thickness of three to four millimeters. You ought to have slices in the form of a rectangle exactly the same size.

Put them in a white cloth and dry them.

When the fat is smoking, plunge the potatoes into it, do not let them stick together nor get golden; shake the basket and let the potatoes fry at full heat for a minute and a half.

Take the pan off the stove, let the boiling of the fat subside; then, quickly, put the pan back on a fierce heat and let the potatoes fry at full heat for half a minute.

Take the basket with the potatoes out of the fat; salt; let them drain while still leaving the frying pan on a brisk heat. Quickly plunge the potatoes back into the fat and take them out at once, letting them drain. The potatoes should puff up instantly. Serve immediately.

$^1/_4$ inch slices.

RICE WITH MUSSELS

RIZ AUX MOULES

In a saucepan put two spoons of olive oil and a good lump of butter; chop very fine an onion, a shallot, a clove of garlic; add a spoon of flour and let it brown slightly.

When it is all nicely golden, moisten with some bouillon, add a quarter of a pound of Carolina rice, a pinch of saffron, salt, and pepper.

Take two pounds of mussels which have been well cleaned, let them open separately in a saucepan and add their liquid to the rice.

Let the rice cook for about twenty to thirty minutes, watching to see that it does not dry out. A quarter of an hour before the cooking of the rice is finished, throw in the mussels without their shells, mix them up well with the rice and serve very hot.

2 Tbs. olive oil, 2 Tbs. butter. Start with 2 cups bouillon, add more as needed to keep just moist.

STUFFED CELERY ROOT (CELERIAC)

CELERI-RAVE FARCI

Take several beautiful, well-rounded celery roots, peel them, and let them blanch in salted water.

When they are lightly cooked and tender, drain them and let them brown lightly with butter to yield up their liquid.

Cut a round on top of the celery root. With a spoon, hollow out the inside and fill it with a stuffing made of meat, sausage meat, and the scrapings of the celery root, seasoned with salt and pepper and *bound* with a béchamel sauce. Close the hole with the round and tie it all up.

Arrange your celery root on a dish which can go into the oven; let it heat and pour over it a yellow sauce called **béarnaise**, as is described in the chapter on sauces. Serve hot.

POTATOES GRATIN

GRATIN DAUPHINOIS

Cut some raw potatoes into rounds of the thickness of an old five-franc piece and lay them on a buttered earthenware dish. Add a little garlic, salt, and pepper. Moisten to the height of the potatoes with milk and spread over them a good piece of fresh butter. Let them cook in a very slow oven.

Slices the size of a silver dollar, or a half crown, cooked 40 min. in a 220° oven.

CHICK PEAS WITH SPINACH

POIS CHICHES AUX EPINARDS

Take some Spanish chick peas, carbenetos, because those of the Midi of France are smaller and harder. Let them soak for at least twenty-four hours in a lot of water, lightly salted. Take the carbenetos out and let them drain.

Fill a soup pot with water, put it on the fire, and when it starts to boil, quickly throw in the chick peas—which is the opposite of what you do with haricot beans. Let them boil continuously but slowly for several hours; when the peas are nearly cooked, take them out and drain them.

In a frying pan put fine olive oil, garlic, tomato and chopped parsley and let them brown.   In another sauce-pan put the liquid in which the peas were cooked, the contents of the frying pan, a few almonds and hazel-nuts, a pinch of saffron, a trace of cinnamon, white, aromatic pepper and cayenne, a hard-boiled egg chop-ped up small and finally the chick peas.

Finish the cooking, watching how the liquid reduces. As a last step put in the whole leaves of the spinach which you have previously blanched and cooked lightly.

Arrange the chick peas in a deep dish with the spinach leaves and rounds of Pamplona sausages, which have barely passed through a frying pan, and coated in the sauce which ought to be creamy.

2 cups dried chick peas or 2 small cans well rinsed. Cook dried beans in $2^1/_2$ cups water about 3 hrs. Just heat canned beans in 1 cup water. Use 3 Tbs. olive oil, 2 to 3 cloves garlic, 3 large peeled tomatoes, 4 Tbs. finely chopped parsley, 8 nuts, 1 lb. spinach, $^1/_2$ lb. garlic sausage.

PARMESAN OF EGGPLANT

PARMESAN D'AUBERGINES

Make a ragout as follows: Cut some beef into pieces, let it brown in butter, and when it is all nicely golden add a little red Chianti or Barolo wine and a few spoon-fuls of purée of tomatoes. While it is cooking moisten it lightly from time to time with warm water.

Menu

Slice the eggplants (aubergines) lengthwise, let them drain with salt, then rinse them in cold water and squeeze them in a white cloth. When the eggplants are dried and drained, brown them in oil.

Garnish a mold with tomato sauce and bread crumbs. Line with slices of eggplant. Then alternate layers of eggplant, grated cheese, slices of hard-boiled eggs, pieces of Italian Provola cheese, little meat balls made with the pieces of beef from the ragout, a little grated crumb of bread, and a little of the sauce from the ragout.

Repeat the layers until the mold is filled and finish with the eggplant and the ragout sauce.

Let it cook gently in the oven.

A good way to use left-over stew in a quantity equal to the amount of eggplant. Use 1 egg per cup of stew.

BROAD FAVA BEANS WITH SAVORY

FEVES A LA SARRIETTE

Have some young fava beans from the peat bogs of the Somme, still green; peel off the first skin, let them cook in water with salt; drain them; then, in a sauté pan put a finger of butter, the broad beans and cream mixed with the finely chopped savory. Salt and pepper to taste; put on a gentle heat so that the cream does not curdle.

This dish can also be made with large fava beans shelled and boiled. These are the fava beans that the Provençals eat raw with salt. With the large cooked beans one has carp.

FOUR-FOLD GRATIN

GRATIN DES QUATRE

In a large well-buttered earthenware dish which can go into the oven make a deep bed of successive layers of round slices of potatoes, rutabaga, celery root, and Jerusalem artichokes, previously scalded, cooked, and drained.

Salt; pepper; and spice strongly; dot with butter and moisten with milk and cream; sprinkle bread crumbs with finely chopped parsley and grated Gruyère cheese.

Put it into a slow oven and let it brown, taking care that the bottom layer does not stick.

Vegetables in equal quantities (peel the artichokes after cooking). Use $^1/_2$ cream, $^1/_2$ milk to barely cover. Bake at least 1 hr. in 325° oven.

GRATIN OF PUMPKIN

GRATIN DE POTIRON

Cut slices of pumpkin half a centimeter thick and as wide as half of your palm. Flour them on both sides and let them cook in a sauté pan with oil, without letting them brown and without putting one on top of another. As they are cooked put them aside on a dish and repeat the process several times.

Separately shred some onions and let them also cook in oil; next treat in the same way some seeded quartered tomatoes, which you will mix, when they have been cooked, with the onion. If you have no fresh tomatoes, use some tomato sauce with the onions which have been cooked but not browned.

In a shallow dish arrange several layers of the slices
of pumpkin, then the mixture of tomatoes and onions,
salt and pepper each layer moderately and finish with
bread crumbs.   Let it brown for a few minutes.

$^1/_4$ inch thick pumpkin slices; $^1/_2$ onion and $^1/_2$ tomato per slice
(or 1 Tbs. tomato sauce).

TOMATOES WITH SHRIMP

TOMATES AUX CREVETTES

Have some nice-looking tomatoes; peel them, cut
them in two through the middle, seed them, and let
them soak in cold water with a little salt.   Place the
halves on a dish, cut sides up, and garnish them with a
layer of freshly milled pepper, green *cornichons*, chopped
fine, and the shelled tails of shrimp.   Cover them all
with a rather thick mayonnaise sauce.   Do not add any
salt as the *cornichons* and shrimp contain enough of it.

EGGPLANT

AUBERGINES

Peel some eggplant like a pear, removing the first
black skin.   Cut them in two lengthwise and slit
through the middle with a knife.   Let them drain with
salt.   Then, put in a stuffing composed of ham, garlic,
parsley, and bread crumbs.   Dot the dish with butter
and put it in the oven.

Stuffing : $^1/_4$ lb. chopped ham, 1 clove garlic, 2 Tbs. chopped
parsley and 2 Tbs. bread crumbs for each medium-sized eggplant.

EGGPLANT

AUBERGINES

Peel some eggplant, cut them in thin slices lengthwise. Salt them and let them drain for two hours. Pat
them dry.

Roll them in flour and let them become transluscent
in a sauté pan with some oil. In a gratin dish, lightly
dotted with butter, arrange a layer of eggplant, then a
layer of fresh minced pork and one of meats, and finish
with a fourth layer of eggplant. Put it in the oven to
cook. Before serving, pour over it a tomato sauce
purée or a spiced thickened sauce.

CHANTERELLES (MUSHROOMS)

GIROLLES

Have some chanterelles and when you have peeled
them, put them in salted water. Let them reduce
completely, add butter, garlic, chopped parsley, and
pepper.

MUSHROOMS WITH CREAM

CHAMPIGNONS A LA CREME

Pick some beautiful meadow mushrooms, or have
some of the cultivated ones called Paris mushrooms.
Peel them, brush them without washing them, and do
not let them get black in the air.

As you clean them throw the mushrooms into a deep
enameled cast-iron pot or into an earthenware sauté

Menu

pan in which there is melted butter. Above all, do not
let them brown. Salt; pepper; cover and let them simmer on a very gentle heat for a quarter of an hour to
twenty-five minutes.   The mushrooms should be
sautéed but not browned. This done, if you used a
saucepan, put the contents—mushrooms and liquid—
into the dish in which the mushrooms are going to be
served. Put the whole in a pan of warm water and pour
over it a generous amount of cream worked with parsley. Let it heat for a quarter of an hour and serve.

2 Tbs. melted butter, $^1/_4$ cup sour cream and 3 Tbs. heavy cream
with 2 Tbs. chopped parsley for each $^1/_2$ lb. of mushrooms.

MORELS (MUSHROOMS)

MORILLES

Take some black mountain morels, which are the most
perfumed and which have a slightly bitter taste. Cut
off the stems and wash or brush them so that the earth
and sand comes away. Wipe them and let them dry in
a white napkin.

Garnish the bottom of an earthenware pot, well
greased with butter, with thick slices of *Paris ham*—
that is to say white ham—not salted and without the
rind.

Add one or two glasses of consommé, according to the
quantity of morels, and a glass of white Bordeaux—a
little fruity like Château Salins or a white Arbois. On
a low flame let them simmer for at least an hour and
a half. Three quarters of an hour before serving,
remove the liquid and make a sauce by *binding* this

liquid with the yolk of an egg and cream. Put what remains of the ham, without any liquid, on a warm dish and cut the ham in pieces on the bottom of the dish. Place the morels on top and pour the cream sauce over it all. Serve hot.

Naturally use a very little salt or pepper, but no garlic or *fines herbes* which might lessen the flavor of the morels.

For $^1/_2$ lb.—morels (3 oz. dried morels, pre-soaked), $^1/_2$ lb. fresh ham, $^3/_4$ to $1^1/_2$ cups consommé, $^3/_4$ cup white wine, 1 egg yolk, $^1/_2$ cup cream.

SALAD WITH BACON FROM ARDENNES

SALADE AU LARD DES ARDENNES

Have some young dandelions from the fields or, as an alternative, some escarole.

Pare, wash and dry the greens carefully in a white cloth.

Into a soup pot put the salad, some boiled, peeled potatoes cut in rounds, two or three spoons of fine olive oil. In a frying pan cook slightly half a pound of small cubes of fat *bacon*. Then heat some wine vinegar in the same pan and add its contents to the soup pot. Finally add a good nut of butter, salt, and ground white pepper.

Put the soup pot on the fire and let it heat gently, uncovered without letting it boil, tossing it to turn the whole mixture over but without breaking the potatoes.

Serve very hot at the beginning of a meal according to the custom in the Ardennes region.

1 lb. of salad greens, 5 medium potatoes peeled, 4 Tbs. wine vinegar, $2^1/_2$ Tbs. butter, for a good-sized group.

WHITE MORELS

MORILLES BLANCHES

Often one has white morels which gourmets disdain. With this recipe one can make the taste of the morel sing.

Having well washed the morels in every corner to remove the sand, let them drain well, dry and wipe them in a white cloth. Cut the morels into a frying pan. Let some butter melt. Sauté the morels and add some small pieces of *Paris ham*, in the proportion of a third of ham to two thirds of morels.

This done, *bind* the whole with an egg yolk, mix in a little *fines herbes*, parsley, but no garlic, onion, etc. Serve hot.

ENGLISH SALAD

SALADE ANGLAISE

Take some tomatoes which have been carefully peeled and seeded and cut them into rounds which you will cover with salt to let the liquid soak out. Have some sausage-type potatoes which have been steamed, cut into rounds, and French beans cooked in water, each cut into four or five pieces.

Mix together the tomatoes without their liquid, the potatoes and French string beans with a mayonnaise sauce, seasoned with salt, vinégar, and Savora mustard. Let it all get well impregnated for two or three hours. At the last moment add some lean York ham, cooked

BORDELAIS BOLETUS (MUSHROOMS)

CEPES BORDELAIS

Wipe the cèpes well, remove the stalks, and put them on the grill so that they yield up their liquid gently.

In an earthenware sauté pan put some oil and let it heat. When the oil is boiling well, throw in the cèpes which will reduce the temperature. When the oil boils again, remove the frying pan to the side of the stove and let it cook on a gentle heat for about one hour.

A quarter of an hour before serving, garnish each mushroom with the stalks, Rocambole, and parsley chopped together. Salt and pepper to taste.

BOLETUS MUSHROOMS FROM THE CAN

CEPES DE CONSERVE

Open a can of cèpes, throw them into a sieve, scald them, and wipe them.

Put into a frying pan one part butter, one part fine oil and let the cèpes brown so that they are a good golden color on each side. Put them to one side.

Peel and set aside the stalks, chop them up with a nut-size lump of dry bread, a shallot, a tiny piece of garlic. Let them brown in butter and garnish the cèpes with this mixture.

In a dish which can go into the oven arrange the cèpes with the mixture on top, sprinkle with bread crumbs worked with *fines herbes*, salt and pepper, and let it cook gently.

Menu

and with very little salt; pour over it a good spoonful of Worcestershire sauce or Chinese sauce. When you have tasted it you can add seasoning or not to the sauce. Then, finally, pour over one or two spoonfuls of fresh cream. Mix the whole well together—the salad should be rich and thick.

For 2 people: 3 med. tomatoes, 2 med. potatoes, $^1/_4$ lb. string beans, $^1/_4$ cup mayonnaise, $^1/_4$ cup cubed ham.

DANDELION SALAD

SALADE DE PISSENLITS

In the fields at the end of January or February, after a thaw, pick some dandelions which are beginning to grow—whose hearts already show signs of yellow.

Wash them and dry them carefully in a cloth. Into a salad bowl put some fine olive oil or fresh walnut oil, let the salt dissolve in it; add some wine vinegar, pepper, and a small spoonful of mustard. Mix it well; crush three or four hard-boiled eggs, finely chopped, and proceed so that the whole mixture is sufficiently seasoned to taste.

Throw in the dandelions and work them for a fairly long time into the sauce. When you are just about to serve, add and toss in a plateful of cubes of bacon, slightly browned and well crisped in butter, and small pieces of red herring.

On a separate plate serve little chapons of the crust of fresh bread rubbed in garlic.

CATALAN SALAD

SALADE CATALANE

For six people prepare:
Two hundred grams of cooked potatoes, two hundred grams of cooked chestnuts, one hundred grams of cooked celery root (celeriac), one hundred grams of cooked red beets. Add fifty grams of shelled walnuts, one hundred grams of sweet apples, two hundred grams of raw Belgian endive, two bananas cut in rounds, fifty grams of shredded Gruyère cheese. Put all these quantities into a salad bowl.

Let the whole steep in good vinegar with salt and pepper for an hour. Make a good mayonnaise and mix everything together.

$^1/_2$ lb. potatoes, $^1/_2$ lb. peeled chestnuts, 1 peeled knob of celery, 2 medium beets, $^1/_4$ cup nut meat, large apple, 2 medium Belgian endive, $^1/_2$ cup cheese.

ABOUT CERTAIN
FLATTERIES

DE QUELQUES FLATTERIES

CREAM AND BACON TART

QUICHE LORRAINE

On a pie plate, lay pastry that you prick and on which you pour a mixture made of three well beaten whole eggs and their volume in fresh cream. Mix in small pieces, as large as peas, of fat *uncured bacon*, about one hundred twenty-five grams. Salt and put in a hot oven.

Remove from the oven when the tart is golden brown and set like baked custard. Serve very hot.

Put 3 eggs in a large measuring cup and note the quantity. Beat eggs; add $^2/_3$ as much cream as there was unbeaten egg. Use $^1/_4$ lb. *uncured bacon*. 30 min. in 400° oven.

BURGUNDIAN CHEESE PASTRY

GOUGERE DE BOURGOGNE

Take twelve eggs, five hundred grams of flour, two hundred fifty grams of butter, one hundred twenty-five grams of Gruyère cut very fine, a tablespoonful of salt, and six glasses of water.

Put the water, salt, and butter into a saucepan and let boil; pour in the flour and simmer for a good quarter of an hour. Add the Gruyère and let it cook for another five minutes.

Pour the contents of the saucepan into a basin, let it cool a little and add the eggs which have been beaten separately.

Work the paste well, until it becomes smooth and firm. Butter a baking sheet and lay the pastry on it,

MENU

spoonful by spoonful. Put it in the oven. At the end of a quarter of an hour, but not before, see if the pastry is cooked. If you open the oven earlier it will not rise.

This is like making cream puff pastry using 1 lb. flour, $^1/_2$ lb. butter, $^1/_4$ lb. Gruyère cheese, 1 tsp. salt, $4^1/_2$ cups water. Lay the spoonfuls so that they touch in a circle. Cook in 400° to 450° oven.

TART FROM CHAMPAGNE

LE TOURTET CHAMPENOIS

Lay out some pastry on a well-buttered pie plate, prick it, and then pour over it three whole eggs beaten into an omelette. Next scatter "choyons" over it, that is to say cubes of *salt pork*, about one hundred twenty-five grams.

Put it in the oven and let it cook until the tart becomes golden brown and crisp. Serve very hot.

$^1/_4$ lb. *salt pork*. 400° oven about 12 min.

SWISS NEUFCHATEL FONDUE

FONDUE DE NEUCHATEL (SUISSE)

Into a heat proof earthenware pot, put a bottle of white wine, a glass of kirsch and half a pound of Emmenthal cheese—that is to say, Gruyère with large eyes—cut in slices. Let it get hot and boil while stirring gently.

When, after about half an hour, the cheese, the wine and the kirsch form a boiling paste, add a dash of aromatic pepper and paprika.

Serve the pot on a lighted spirit burner in the middle of the table, with a plate of croutons sautéed in butter. Each guest will dip a crouton into the fondue which continues to boil until it is used up.

At the end, one retains the bottom of the fondue and lets it brown until it becomes very dark. This last "gratinage," of which each guest eats a mouthful, is incomparable.

To accompany it, a wine from Arbois, Yvorne, Fendant, or a Blanc de Blanc from Champagne.

This fondue was made on returning from chamois hunts in the Dead Plain, Canton Valais.

Use ³/₄ cup kirsch. Begin heating gently till boil is reached.

CHEESE RACLETTE

RACLETTE DE FROMAGE

Take the half or a quarter of a wheel of Tomme, cheese of the High Alps. Pierce this piece with a long-handled iron fork and present the cut side to a clear fire of pine wood.

When the cheese begins to melt, scrape it with a wooden knife and lay a boiling round of it—of five to eight centimeters—on the plates, placed on charcoal heaters. Salt lightly and pepper.

Accompany these rounds of melted cheese, called raclettes, with potatoes grilled in the ashes, and with red Fendant wine or any other wine which has a taste of gunflint. Devour as many raclettes as you can.

This dish is recommended to chamois hunters and to alpinists who, after several days in the high mountains, come back in a state of exhaustion, wanting only to drink and unable to swallow any solid food such as bread or meat.

2 inch to 3 inch boiling rounds.

WELSH RAREBIT
A small rare morsel from Wales
UN PETIT MORCEAU RARE GALLOIS

Take a loaf of soft-crusted bread and make toast (slices of bread) of half a centimeter thick; butter them on both sides, and put them on a dish which can go into the oven. Set aside.

In a copper saucepan put some grated Cheddar cheese, moisten it with pale ale, let it melt on a gentle fire. Add English Worcester sauce and cayenne pepper, stirring continuously with a wooden spoon until it becomes the consistency of a thick mayonnaise.

Pour the paste over the toast, put the dish into the oven, and let it brown.

$^1/_4$ inch thick slices of white toast. About 1 cup ale for each pound of cheese. Place under broiler or use 550° oven.

CHEESE BREAD TO GIVE YOU A THIRST
PAIN DE FROMAGE POUR BIEN BOIRE

Mix one hundred twenty-five grams of flour, seventy-five grams of grated cheese—Gruyère or Parmesan—salt and cayenne pepper, half a coffee spoon of Alsatian yeast.   When you have kneaded it all together, add seventy-five grams of butter and the yolk of an egg.

Lay out the paste, cut it in strips or rounds, glaze with an egg yolk, put it in a hot oven for about ten minutes.

$^3/_4$ cup flour, $^3/_4$ cup cheese, $^1/_2$ tsp. yeast, $^1/_3$ cup butter (cut in). Buttered baking sheet in 400° oven.

GALICHE FROM CHAMPAGNE

GALICHE CHAMPENOIS

In a porcelain dish which can go into the oven, at least five centimeters deep, lay some tart pastry, over which you pour the following mixture: two spoons of flour, half a liter of fresh cream, three whole eggs, salt, and sugar.

Mix the flour with one part of milk, add the salt and sugar and, while stirring, incorporate the eggs, one by one, and then the cream.

Put into a hot oven.   The tart should be very golden. Sprinkle with sugar and serve very hot.

Porcelain plate at least 2 inches deep.   2 Tbs. flour, $1^1/_2$ cups heavy cream, $^1/_2$ cup sour cream, 4 Tbs. sugar.   Begin by mixing flour to a paste with 2 Tbs. milk.   400° oven 25 min.

BEEF MARROW TART

TARTE A LA MOELLE

In a flame-proof porcelain pie dish, thirty centimeters in diameter, lay out some pastry as for an ordinary tart.

Pour over it the mixture prepared thus:

MENU

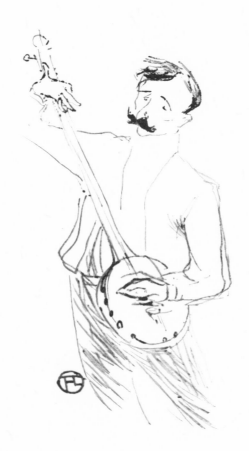

In a terrine put a quarter of a pound of granulated sugar and a tablespoon of powdered cinnamon. Stir, while adding two whole eggs, previously beaten, and two glasses of raw warm milk, then a quarter of a pound of beef marrow which has been melted in a double boiler with a little butter and strained. Cook in a moderate oven.

12 inch pie plate (Pyrex). 2 cups sugar, $1^1/_2$ cups light cream. To obtain marrow, simmer beef marrow bones 1 hr. in salted water; scoop out marrow. To prepare, place marrow (about $^1/_4$ cup) in heavy saucepan with 1 Tbs. butter; cook gently 15 min.; serve. Cook tart 40 min. in 325° oven.

FRUIT TART

TARTE AUX FRUITS

To make a good fruit tart, prepare the pastry the night before with wheaten flour—on guard not to handle it too much—in the proportions of a third of butter to two thirds of flour; add sufficient water and salt.

Cover with a cloth and let your pastry rest.

Next day, lay it out; add a little more butter, roll it and fold it many and many a time.

Bed your pastry on a buttered baking sheet; prick it with a fork so that it does not puff up when cooking, otherwise you will have puff pastry.

Next set out your fruit: cherries, cherry plums, mirabelle plums, various stoned plums, apples cut in rounds, sugar according to the acidity of your fruit.

And, to decorate, with some pastry, place your initials on top; for example, "Momo." *

* A pet pseudonym for Lautrec.

APPLE TARTOUILLAT

TARTOUILLAT AUX POMMES

This dish is extremely delicate to make because cooks always tend to put in too many apples and too much pastry: this dish resembles neither a turnover nor an apple tart.

Have two flame-proof pie dishes in wrought iron whose sides are not fluted, one dish larger than the other.

In the smaller dish put first of all a very thick layer of butter and, above it, a very thick layer of granulated sugar. Then add a layer of cider apples cut in very thin slices and packed tight in one thickness. It would be better, so as not to have any chinks, to make squares and lozenge shapes to fill the bottom of the dish entirely.

On this bed of apples, put a layer of granulated sugar and a light layer of butter. On the dish thus prepared, lay a very thin layer, like a leaf of paper, of tart pastry, taking great care not to make any rim on the pastry.

Put the dish in the oven, placed on two bricks, until it begins to caramelize. When it is all almost completely cooked, turn it out into the larger dish, spread with butter and sugar, and put it back in the oven, in such a way that the pastry comes underneath.

Finish the cooking so that the whole is caramelized.

Serve in the boiling hot dish, cutting the tartouillat into squares. All the sugar, apples and pastry should be mingled one with the other to form a sort of soft caramel with apples.

Bake in 450° oven on wire rack.

RUM TART

TARTE AU RHUM

In a well-buttered pie dish lay out a pastry that you dot generously with butter. Sprinkle it heavily with sugar and pour over it a glass of liquid made up of three quarters of good rum and one quarter of water.

Put in a very hot oven and serve warm.

3 Tbs. butter, 5 Tbs. sugar, $1/2$ cup rum, $1/4$ cup water. 500° oven till crust is golden. Let tart cool slightly.

ALMOND TART

TARTE AUX AMANDES

On some tart pastry lay the following mixture prepared overnight:

Half a pound of almonds which have been peeled, cut into the smallest pieces possible, and put into a bowl in layers alternating with granulated sugar and moistened from time to time with water scented with orange flowers. Put it into a gentle oven.

275° oven until crust is golden brown.

FRANGIPANE TART

TARTE FRANGIPANE

Onto some tart pastry pour the following mixture:
Work one hundred twenty-five grams of flour with four eggs; then add a liter of warm milk, a little salt,

two hundred fifty grams of granulated sugar, forty grams of orange-flower water. When the mixture is finished, add thirty shelled almonds cut in slices. Pour over the pastry and cook in a moderate oven; unmold and serve warm.

Use a high spring tart ring. $^3/_4$ cup flour, 4 cups milk, 1 scant cup sugar, 2 Tbs. orange-flower water.

LEMON TART

TARTE AU CITRON

Lay some tart pastry on an open pie dish, covering the sides. Pour over it the following mixture:

Beat three whole eggs as for an omelette, add their weight in granulated sugar, the juice of a lemon and its grated zest, and seventy grams of butter cut into small pieces.

Put into a moderate oven.

$^3/_4$ cup sugar, $^1/_3$ cup butter. 375° oven for 20 minutes.

STRAWBERRY AND RASPBERRY TART

TARTE AUX FRAISES ET AUX FRAMBOISES

In a well-buttered dish lay some pastry that you prick. Fill it with beans or well-washed pebbles. Let the pastry cook without getting dry.

When the pastry is quite cold, take out the beans or the stones which were used to keep the shape, pour over it four whites of egg beaten to snow; incorporate one

Menu

weight in pounded sugar. Let them soak for twenty-four hours, then put them back on the fire. Let them boil and add one small glass of rum per pound of fruit when you take them off the fire.

After first cooking 2 lbs. of plums, put in water to cover with 2 lbs. granulated sugar. Boil in this liquid. Then, add ³/₄ cup rum.

CHOCOLATE MAYONNAISE

MAYONNAISE AU CHOCOLAT

In a saucepan put four bars of chocolate with very little water and let them melt on a very gentle fire. Add four large spoons of granulated sugar, half a pound of good butter, four yolks of eggs and mix carefully.

Let it cool and you will have a smooth paste. Beat the whites of eggs to a snow and mix them, while stirring, into the paste.

A variation on mousse. ¹/₂ lb. semi-sweet chocolate, 4 heaping Tbs. sugar.

ORANGE PRESERVE

CONFITURE D'ORANGES

Take some oranges with thick skins, peel them lightly and put them one by one into fresh water; next, plunge them into boiling water and leave them there for about a quarter of an hour until you can easily pass a pin's head through. Drain them and cut them into quarters, taking care to remove the pips.

Make a syrup, which you will allow to cook for about an hour. When it is smooth, put in the oranges and let them cook for about three hours—one can tell that the quarters are sufficiently cooked when the skin becomes transparent. To one pound of fruit one needs to add a pound and a quarter of sugar and a liter and a quarter of water.

To 1 lb. fruit, 3 cups sugar, 5 cups water.

PEARS COOKED IN RED WINE

POIRES CUITES AU VIN ROUGE

Peel your pears. Seed them and if they are large, cut them in two; if not, leave them whole.

In a saucepan put half a liter of liquid—that is, two thirds wine and one third water for two pounds of pears—four hundred grams of sugar and half a clove.

Let them cook until the pears become scarlet and the syrup thick.

$1^1/_3$ cup wine, $^2/_3$ cup water, 2 lbs. pears, $1^3/_4$ cups sugar.   Simmer.

CASSIS

Take a wide-mouthed jar holding several liters (four); fill it three quarters full with black currants well-plucked from their stalks. Add a light layer of raspberries, a black currant leaf, and a small piece of stick cinnamon.

Fill the jar to cover the contents with good quality white eau-de-vie so that the black currants are soaking and that the eau-de-vie rises above it by a quarter.

Seal the jar hermetically with a folded cloth, a stopper or a saucer. Let it steep for at least three months —at most six months. Pour the liquor into a vessel through a sieve.

Crush the berries and press them in a cloth the better to extract the juice; mix it well together with the first juice.

Filter successively with a funnel and filter papers. Fill some liter bottles to measure the quantity.

This done, pour the liquor filtered into the bottles back into a clean vessel and add half a pound of sugar per liter of juice. Let it dissolve, mix well, return to the bottles and seal hermetically.

RUM PUNCH

PUNCH AU RHUM

In a copper saucepan put a liter of water, four pounds of sugar, and the whole zests of two lemons. Let them boil well, take out the zests and let the liquid cool.

Throw the cold syrup into a vessel with two and a half liters of rum and half a liter of very strong tea.

Mix and put into a bottle to serve the punch hot or cold.

Syrup: 4 cups water, 4 lbs. sugar. Punch: 10 cups rum, 2 cups tea.

FRESH CURRANT SALAD

SALADE DE GROSEILLES

Put into a basin three parts of red currants, one part of white currants—well plucked from their stalks—and one part of raspberries.

Cover generously with sugar and moisten with a very little vinegar.

Let them steep for at least twelve hours, stirring from time to time. Several hours before serving, add some kirsch according to your taste.

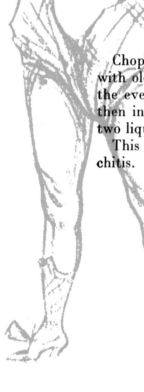

PORT WITH GARLIC

PORTO A L'AIL

Chop a pound of garlic, put it into a liter bottle filled with old port and let it steep for twenty days. Begin the evening with half a liqueur glass before the soup, then increase the dosage, little by little, up to one or two liqueur glasses.

This brew is a sovereign remedy for chronic bronchitis.

MENU

CERTAIN MENUS

Salad with Ardennes ham   Dish of stuffed tomatoes
Jellied pike with red wine   Dish of stuffed mushrooms
Thrushes en cocotte   Shrimps à la nage
Tarts with cherry plums   Lemon tart (or open pie)
Cheese   Roquefort cheese
Dessert   Dessert, fruit, etc.

Pot-au-feu, cold consommé
Boiled beef, short ribs, with marrow bones
Salt pork with vegetables from the pot-au-feu
Dish of pork sausages
Dish of glazed onions

Raised duck pie   Veal Marengo
Stewed veal   Asparagus sauce mousseline
Pâté of mock rabbit   Lark pâté pie
Endive salad   Lettuce salad
Rum tart   Marrowbone tart
Brie cheese   Roblochon cheese
Dessert   Dessert

Large sole with tarragon
Wild duck with carrots and olives
Mushrooms with cream
Mademoiselle Tatin's apple tart
Goat cheese from Touraine and the Orléanais
Dessert

Lobster à l'Américaine
Roast veal
Cooked endive
Strawberry and raspberry tart
Camembert cheese
Dessert

Burgundian cheese pastry
A whole roast partridge per guest
Potatoes fried en rabot
Pâtés de foie gras in a crust
Endive salad
Plum tarts
Port Salut cheese
Dessert

Menu of Miss May Belfort, 1896

Oxtail soup
Hors-d'œuvre
Lake Michigan trout
Haunch of venison on a purée of chestnuts
Foie gras in a crust
Salad
Sweet course
Dessert
Grand table wine—Vouvray, Corton

Formula for Two Courses

To the two courses add vegetables, salads, sweet dishes, tarts, cheeses as preferred. Fruit and dessert optional.

Brill, white sauce with capers
Wild duck with carrots and olives

Sauerkraut with champagne and preserved goose
Roast pheasant

Chicken with almonds
Boar's head with pistachio

Veal cutlets on endive
Pâté of duck from the Somme in a crust

Catfish grilled over the embers
with sprigs of fennel
Salmi of scoter duck

Calf liver with dried plums
Pâté of mock rabbit

Beef with Malromé red wine
Roast wood pigeon on croutons

Menu

Neck of mutton with potatoes
Galantine of poultry

Grilled shad on a bed of young sorrel
Braised Auvergne leg of mutton

Picardy pike with red wine
Stuffed shoulder of veal rolled in vegetables

Trout with cream
Calves' liver with juniper and ham

Shrimps
Cassoulet

Burgundy snails
Goose stuffed with blood sausage

Stewed eel with white wine
Roast ribs of beef

Roast and stuffed pike of fifteen pounds
Roast partridges

Large sole with tarragon
Chicken with cream

Stewed veal
Roast woodcock

Sheep's trotters poulette
Boar's head

Roast turkey stuffed with blood sausage
and chestnuts
Prague ham in a crust

Red cabbage with chestnuts
Thrushes with juniper

Trout under the ashes stuffed with shrimps
Pâté of hare in a crust

Arroz à la Valenciana
Jellied pike with red wine

Chicken with rice and curry
Roast haunch of wild boar

Brill with red wine and gooseberries
Roast wild rabbit with olives

Bouillabaisse
Roast snipe

Lobster à l'Américaine
Roast veal

Raised pie with goose or duck
Cold jellied beef à la mode

MENU

GRASSHOPPERS GRILLED IN THE FASHION OF SAINT JOHN THE BAPTIST

SAUTERELLES GRILLEES A LA MODE DE SAINT JEAN-BAPTISTE

From a large swarm of grasshoppers, choose the most beautiful, the pink rather than the brown or the yellow.

Put them on a screen and let them grill lightly over a charcoal fire while at the same time sprinkling them with a few pinches of coarse salt.

Tear off the head by turning them so that the whole digestive tract will come out intact.

Lay the grasshoppers on a dish garnished with rounds of lemon; season to taste with salt and ordinary and red pepper.

Shell and eat the desert grasshoppers (locusts) in the same way as "grasshoppers" of the English Channel, that is to say shrimps, which have the same savor.

SAINT ON THE GRILL

SAINT SUR LE GRIL

With the help of the Vatican try to procure for yourself a real(!) saint.

Treat him as St. Lawrence was treated on August tenth, A.D. 258. When you have whipped him, lay him on the grill over a big bed of charcoal. Like his predecessor, if he is a real saint, he himself will ask to be turned over in order to be grilled to a turn on both sides.

ANCIENT RECIPE

Full of mystery. It will never be known.

God revealed the knowledge only to his Prophet, who uttered no word about it. This recipe will, therefore, remain forever unknown to all other human beings.

ULTIMA RATIO FINIS

Menu

INDEX

This book was produced by
EDITA S. A. LAUSANNE

It was printed in letterpress (text and drawings)
by Imprimerie Centrale Lausanne S. A.,
and in offset (inserts)
by Imprimerie Paul Attinger S. A., Neuchâtel.

The edition was bound
by Maurice Busenhart, Lausanne.

Printed in Switzerland